# Study Skills

The complete guide to smart learning

GALORE PARK

# Study Skills

The complete guide to smart learning

Elizabeth Holtom

Published by Galore Park Publishing Ltd
19/21 Sayers Lane, Tenterden, Kent TN30 6BW
www.galorepark.co.uk

Text copyright © Elizabeth Holtom 2007
Illustrations copyright © Galore Park 2007
The 3D cartoons used in this book are © www.animationfactory.com
Cover illustration by Gwyneth Williamson

Typography, design and layout by Design Gallery, Suffolk
Printed and bound by Replika Press, India

ISBN-13: 978 1 902984 59 9

First published 2007, reprinted January 2008, December 2008, 2009

Details of other Galore Park Publications are available at www.galorepark.co.uk

ISEB Revision Guides, publications and examination papers may also be obtained from Galore Park.

# About the author

Elizabeth Holtom graduated from London University with a Combined Honours Degree in French and German and then gained a postgraduate Certificate of Education from Cambridge University.   She began her career teaching French to A level at James Allen's Girls' School in London, where she became joint Head of Sixth Form.  After a career break to raise a young family, she resumed teaching French. When she discovered that one of her sons was dyslexic, she decided to study for the RSA Diploma in Specific Learning Difficulties at the Helen Arkell Dyslexia Centre, Frensham.  Since 1994 she has taught pupils with special needs at all levels.  She has held the position of Learning Support Co-ordinator at Cranleigh Prep School and is now their Study Skills Co-ordinator.  She runs study skills courses for students preparing for Common Entrance and continues to teach pupils with specific learning difficulties.

# Acknowledgements

I am grateful to everyone who has contributed, both professionally and personally, to this book with their comments, ideas and support.  These include the many students I have taught over the years and the teachers who have shared their professional expertise with me and tried out my ideas.

In particular, I wish to thank my family for their encouragement and patience, Jane Mitchell of CALSC (Communication and Learning Skills Centre) and my children's study skills teacher, for providing the inspiration to develop my interest in study skills. I also wish to thank all those students who have participated in my study skills courses and have given me invaluable feedback and personal contributions. My colleagues at Cranleigh Prep School have also been of immense help: Michael Roulston, Headmaster, for his belief in the value of study skills; Emily McGhee, Learning Support Co-ordinator for her encouragement and advice. I also wish to acknowledge other staff, for sharing their specialist expertise with me: James Adcock (Geography), Toby Batchelor (Religious Studies), Robin Gainher (History), Mark Halstead (Latin), Alison Jolly (Science), Jude Marriott (English), Janet Roulston (Food Technology). In addition I would like to thank Lindy Bates, Learning Support Co-ordinator at Marlborough House Prep School and Louise Martine of Galore Park Publishing who helped me develop this book from first draft to finished article.

The author and publisher gratefully acknowledge Jane Mitchell's permission to cite her practical work on breaks and the reviewing method in Exercise 1.6 which she devised.

# Contents

* Note: MIND MAPS® is a registered trademark of the Buzan Organisation Ltd
www.buzanworld.com, tony.buzan@buzanworld.com

# Introduction

Study Skills: The complete guide to smart learning offers you a fantastic opportunity to find out how you learn and how to make the best possible use of the time you spend studying. Follow this step-by-step guide and discover the way to boost your grades in tests and examinations.

## Author's note to students

This is a very special guide to learning because you will make it your own, personal handbook. There are three ways for you to make this possible.

### Exercises
Carry out all the exercises because each one has a vital part to play in making you a smart learner. Some will help you find out how you learn and others will train you in the skills you need for smart learning.

### I promise
Look out for the 'I promise' boxes. You will check the section you have just read and then choose how to put your smart learning into practice. Every reader will make different promises because everyone has his or her special way of learning.

### Feedback for you
After a break of several days or weeks you will decide how well you are doing at keeping your promises. Give yourself a grade for progress:

I am keeping my promises

A all the time ☐     B most of the time ☐     C some of the time ☐     D never ☐

Only move on to the next section of the book once you have achieved an A or B.

There are three other important parts of the book you should make the most of.

### Tips
These are useful pieces of advice based on the experience of students I have taught.

### Watch out!
Look out for the warnings. These are also based on the experience of students who have taken examinations before you.

## Summaries

There is a summary at the end of each section. This is a useful way for you to check over what you have just read about before moving on to the next section.

I recommend the following approach to your reading:

1. Read the contents page so that you have an overview of what the whole book is about.

2. Read the book in small, manageable chunks.

3. Read the chapters in the order they are written. You will build up your understanding of yourself first and develop your skills next.

4. Do the **exercises** and make your **promises** as you come to them.

5. Fill in the **Feedback for you** boxes in pencil. A high score means you are ready to move on. A low score means you have more work to do before moving on. Rub out your score once it has improved, change it and move on.

6. Read the summaries to remind yourself of the key points in each section.

7. Make reading this guide fun and transform it into your personal handbook!

I hope you will continue to find this guide useful for all the tests and exams you will take. Dip into it whenever you want to remind yourself how your amazing brain works and how to use the fantastic techniques you are about to become an expert in.

# Author's note to parents and teachers

My aim with this book is to take your children/students on an exciting voyage of discovery about themselves and how they learn. I have kept the theory behind how they learn to a minimum. However, there is much more to explore in the whole area of brain-based learning. The bibliography at the back is by no means exhaustive, but includes a selection of reference books that have inspired me and resource materials I find very useful.

When I run a study skills workshop I tell students I am like a chef, not a doctor. This book is not a prescriptive list of what you should and shouldn't do. It is a buffet from which students should choose what suits them best. However, you are definitely the assistant chefs! Students of this age will need practical help and encouragement if they are to succeed in establishing good studying habits. The more these habits are practised at home and in the classroom, the better. Your support in helping them become smart learners will be invaluable.

# All about you

## 1.1 Your amazing brain

Clench your two fists and hold them next to each other. This is about the size of your brain. Scientists believe it contains more than one hundred billion neurons or brain cells. You learn by making connections between neurons. Your brain is capable of more connections than there are atoms in the known universe. Yes, it really is amazing!

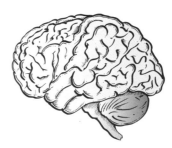

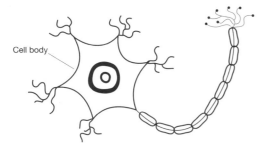

Cell body

A neuron

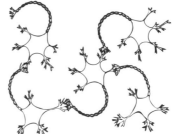

Neurons connecting with other neurons. Everytime you learn something more connections are made!

### Look after your brain

Your brain is really special so it makes sense to find out how to look after it.

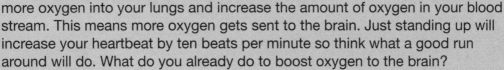

● **Get plenty of exercise**
Believe it or not, your brain is greedy.

It is only about 2% of your body weight, but it uses 20% of the oxygen energy that you produce. Your brain needs lots and lots of oxygen to keep it working well.

The best way to boost your oxygen levels is by getting plenty of exercise. All that deep breathing you have to do when you run around will force more oxygen into your lungs and increase the amount of oxygen in your blood stream. This means more oxygen gets sent to the brain. Just standing up will increase your heartbeat by ten beats per minute so think what a good run around will do. What do you already do to boost oxygen to the brain?

● **Eat a healthy diet**
Smart learners know how important it is to eat a brain-friendly diet to help boost their grades. On the next page are some of the things on their menu. Make sure your diet is brain-friendly too.

## Brain-friendly dishes of the day
Here are a few dishes for you to choose from.

Breakfast

Homemade muesli with grains, seeds and dried fruit
Add yogurt/milk
Porridge topped with dried fruit and honey
Eggs – poached/boiled – with multi-grain toast
Banana and apple smoothies

Snacks

Dried fruit/fresh fruit
Toast and peanut butter
Mixed nuts and raisins
Blueberry/cranberry cookies

Lunch/supper

Spinach and noodle soup
Spaghetti with sun-dried tomatoes, basil and pine nuts
Salmon fish cakes with a couscous salad
Tuna and grated carrot salad
Caesar salad
Sesame beef stir fry
Lean beefburgers with a bulgar wheat salad
BBQ lamb pizza on a wholemeal base with green salad
Fresh fruit salad with dried fruits, seeds and natural yogurt

## Watch out!
Junk food full of additives will damage your concentration. Sugar-coated breakfast cereals will give you a quick energy burst but are followed by a much longer energy slump. Fizzy drinks are rich in sugar too and can make you hyperactive. This will block concentration. So, if you love this kind of food and drink, keep them for a treat for the times when you are not learning.

Dehydration will also damage your concentration. Make sure you drink plenty of water while you are studying.

### Think positively

You want to get the best out of your brain so you must become a positive, can-do student. Your brain is very trusting. It believes what you tell it.

Tell yourself you are a great student who is going to do well. Your brain will believe you.

Tell your brain 'I can't do this' and it will believe that instead.

Even when you have something tough to learn, tell your brain 'I can do this but I am going to need a little help.'

Give your brain positive messages so it will want to study.

### Exercise 1.1: Positive thinking

Here's a good way to train yourself to think positively:

1. Think of an activity you really enjoy.

2. Close your eyes or look up.

3. Picture yourself enjoying this activity.

4. Notice how good you feel – focus on that warm glow you have inside you.

5. Picture yourself walking into the room where you are going to take a test or exam.

6. Keep that warm glow inside as you smile and look calmly at the paper, knowing you are ready to do your best.

Positive thinking gets the best out of your brain. Be proud of all of your successes and enjoy that warm feeling you get inside.

### Keep calm

Your brain is very sensitive. It can cope with small amounts of stress. Indeed, a little stress can produce just the right amount of adrenaline to help you finish a project on time, learn for that test or be ready for exams. However, large amounts of stress are bad for it. Have you ever thought 'My mind has gone blank'? This means your thinking brain has shut down because it is under too much stress. So make sure that you keep calm.

## Exercise 1.2: How to keep calm

Here is a relaxation exercise to help keep you calm.

1. Sit comfortably with your feet on the floor, legs uncrossed. Let your shoulders drop to help you relax.

2. Shut your eyes.

3. Put your hands on your stomach and take a steady breath. Feel your stomach push out as you start to fill your lungs. Count to four as you breathe in.

4. Breathe out slowly through your mouth. Count to four as you breathe out.

5. Make sure your breathing is regular and calm. Breathe in and out three or four times.

This exercise has the bonus of giving your brain an excellent oxygen boost.

---

- **Take breaks**

  Keep your brain fresh and alert by taking regular breaks during your study time. After 20 minutes of learning, do some stretches – the kind you might do as a warm-up for sport. Or you might learn how to juggle. Juggling is an excellent break activity. These activities will improve blood flow, relax your body and reduce tension.

- **Get enough sleep**

  Your brain needs to be fresh for a new day of studies so give it the good night's sleep it deserves. Your brain is switched on all the time – even when you are asleep. It actually carries on sorting out what you have learnt whilst you are happily sleeping. That good night's sleep will really pay off because it will help you learn.

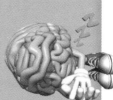

---

I promise

How do you promise to look after your amazing brain?

**1.** I shall get plenty of exercise by .............................................................

.............................................................

**2.** My brain-friendly diet will include .............................................................

.............................................................

**3.** I shall use my positive thinking routine

Before school starts ☐          At the end of the day ☐

**4.** I shall use a relaxation exercise

Before I start revising ☐          Before a test or exam ☐

**5.** I shall give my brain a break by ...............................................................

...........................................................................................................

**6.** I shall go to bed at ...........................during term time

---

**Take a break**

You have made up to six very important promises. Spend several days making them come true before you carry on reading.

---

**How smart are you becoming?**

Give yourself a grade and only carry on reading when you are happy with your score.

• I am looking after my brain:

A all the time ☐     B most of the time ☐     C some of the time ☐     D never ☐

## Understand your thinking brain

Your thinking brain is the part that looks a bit like a wrinkled walnut. It is called the **neo-cortex**. Clench one fist. Now wrap your other hand round your fist to make it into the neo-cortex. The **neo-cortex** is two millimetres thick and, if it were spread out, would be the size of an open newspaper. That explains why it looks so wrinkled: it has been squeezed up to fit inside your skull.

Your thinking brain is made up of two parts called the left and right hemispheres. They are joined together by the **corpus callosum**. This acts like a telephone exchange, sending messages from one hemisphere to the other. The two hemispheres work together in a very complex way. However, each hemisphere has a different way of sorting out information. Think of doing a jigsaw. It helps to look at the picture on the box so you know what you are aiming for. This gives you the **big picture**. You also need to notice all the small changes of colour and shape that help you choose which pieces are going to fit together. This gives you the **detail**. The **right hemisphere** of your brain sorts out the **big picture** and the **left hemisphere** sorts out the **detail** when you are learning. You need both for smart learning. Find out next how your brain likes to think.

## Exercise 1.3: Understand your thinking brain

Look at the exercise below. Every time you agree with a statement, put a tick in the box next to it. You can tick as many boxes as you like.

**Odds and evens**

1. I like to move around. People say I am a fidget in class! ☐

2. I find it easy to sit still and listen to the teacher and do my work. ☐

3. I like group work. ☐

4. I like to work on my own. ☐

5. I can give the right answer to a maths problem but cannot tell you how I got it. ☐

6. I always show my workings in mathematics. ☐

7. Learning tables is difficult. ☐

8. Learning tables is easy. ☐

9. I find spelling difficult. ☐

10. I find spelling easy. ☐

11. I use words like 'Um' or 'Er' a lot when I am talking and change the subject. ☐

12. I enjoy speaking in class and can stick to the point. ☐

13. I enjoy subjects where I can paint and use colour. ☐

14. I enjoy subjects where I can write and use words. ☐

15. I am often late finishing my work. ☐

16. I finish my work on time. ☐

17. My desk and locker are messy. ☐

18. My desk and locker are tidy. ☐

19. I like making things using my own ideas. ☐

20. I like to follow step-by-step instructions when making something. ☐

21. I pay more attention to the tune of a song than its lyrics. ☐

22. I pay more attention to the words in a song than its tune. ☐

Use the picture of the neo-cortex on the opposite page to work out your score. Put a tick in all the boxes where the number matches one you have ticked in the questionnaire.

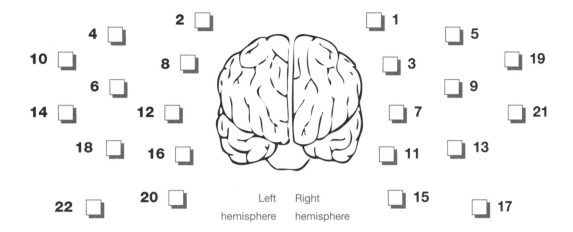

Now add up your scores for each hemisphere.

My left hemisphere score is ………    My right hemisphere score is ………

• Is your left hemisphere score higher? This means you have a left-brain thinking style. You are a step-by-step learner and you enjoy words.

• Is your right hemisphere score higher? This means you have a right-brain thinking style. You are a big picture learner and you enjoy pictures.

• Are you balanced between the two? This means you have a combination thinking style.

There is no right or wrong answer. What is important is that you make the most of your thinking strengths when you are learning.

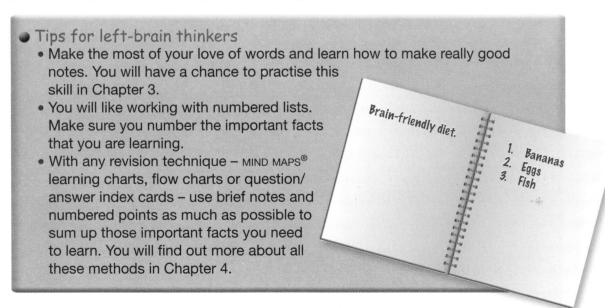

● Tips for left-brain thinkers
  • Make the most of your love of words and learn how to make really good notes. You will have a chance to practise this skill in Chapter 3.
  • You will like working with numbered lists. Make sure you number the important facts that you are learning.
  • With any revision technique – MIND MAPS® learning charts, flow charts or question/answer index cards – use brief notes and numbered points as much as possible to sum up those important facts you need to learn. You will find out more about all these methods in Chapter 4.

Brain-friendly diet.

1. Bananas
2. Eggs
3. Fish

- You are likely to prefer a quiet place to work in.
- You like to keep on track with everything you have to do at school, so make the most of the planners on the Galore Park website. You will find out more about these in Chapter 2.

● Tips for right-brain thinkers

- Make the most of your love of colour and pictures and learn how to turn key words into pictures. You will have a chance to practise this skill in Chapter 4.
- You will enjoy learning charts because your brain likes having all the information on one sheet of paper.
- With any revision technique – MIND MAPS® learning charts, flow charts or question/answer index cards – use colour and pictures as much as possible to sum up those important facts you need to learn. You will find out more about all these methods in Chapter 4.
- You may enjoy having music playing in the background while you study. More about music in Section 2.3 on page 30.
- You need to use the planners available for download from the Galore Park website. You will learn more about how to use them in Chapter 2. You may not want to use them, but you really must, as you tend to be pretty disorganised!

I promise

How are you going to make the most of your amazing brain?

**1.** Look at your higher score first and choose from the tips that match this kind of thinker.

(a) I shall make the most of my left-brain strengths by ...................................

........................................................................................................

Or

(b) I shall make the most of my right-brain strengths by ...............................

........................................................................................................

**2.** Now look at your lower score and choose from the tips that match this kind of thinker.

(a) I shall build up my left-brain thinking by ...............................................

........................................................................................................

Or

(b) I shall build up my right-brain thinking by ..............................................

........................................................................................................

**Take a break**

You have made some more very important promises. Spend several days making them come true before you carry on reading.

**How smart are you becoming?**
Give yourself a grade and only carry on reading when you are happy with your score.

- I am making the most of my left/right-brain strengths:

  A all the time ☐    B most of the time ☐    C some of the time ☐    D never ☐

- I am building up my left/right-brain thinking

  A all the time ☐    B most of the time ☐    C some of the time ☐    D never ☐

# Summary: Your amazing brain

### Smart learners look after their brains
- They give their brain plenty of oxygen by exercising.
- They eat brain-friendly food.
- They think in a can-do way.
- They keep calm by using a relaxation exercise.
- They take regular breaks during their study time.
- They make sure they get enough sleep.

### Smart learners understand their brains
- The neo-cortex is the thinking part of the brain.
- Left-brain thinking is step-by-step and focuses on the detail.
- My left-brain thinking score was ..................... .
- Right-brain thinking sees whole patterns and focuses on the big picture.
- My right-brain thinking score was ......................... .
- We need both to be smart learners.

# 1.2 Learn how you learn

Making the most of your senses makes you a smart learner.

Think back to when you were a toddler. Your mother needed eyes in the back of her head! Why? Everything you could get your hands on was so interesting that you would look at it, feel it, listen to it, smell it and, yes, end up putting it in your mouth. You were using all your senses to learn.

At school you learn by looking, listening and doing. These are your three main learning channels. You will use all three but it is quite likely that you will have one or even two favourites. These are your learning preferences. The good news is that the better you understand your preferences the easier it will be to become a smart learner.

## Exercise 1.4: How you like to learn

Complete this exercise to find out how you like to learn. Read about the following situations. Choose the answer that is best for you and tick the relevant box A, B or C.

1. You are going to visit a friend for the first time. Which instructions on how to get there help you the most?
   - [ ] A. Your friend gives you a map.
   - [ ] B. Your friend goes with you the first time to show you the way.
   - [ ] C. Your friend explains on the phone how you get there.

2. Your mother is cooking sausages for supper. Which do you notice most?
   - [ ] A. The sizzling of the sausages as they fry.
   - [ ] B. The way the sausages burst and change colour as they fry.
   - [ ] C. The fact that you are feeling hungry and are looking forward to your supper.

3. You have gone bowling with your friends. Which do you notice most?
   - [ ] A. The rumble of the bowling balls rolling down the alley and the crash as the pins fall down.
   - [ ] B. The movement as you swing your arm and let the heavy bowling ball go.
   - [ ] C. The size and colour of the bowling ball you have chosen.

4. You are walking by the sea. Which do you notice most?
   - [ ] A. The sunlight sparkling on the sea.
   - [ ] B. The sound of the waves breaking on the shore.
   - [ ] C. The cold water splashing over your feet.

**5.** You meet your friends in town. Which do you pay attention to first of all?

☐ A. Your feeling of pleasure at being with your friends.

☐ B. The voices of your friends as they chat to you.

☐ C. The faces of your friends as they smile at you.

**6.** You have a new CD player and have to assemble the shelves that it will sit on. How do you set about it?

☐ A. You unpack the shelves and start trying to put them up straightaway.

☐ B. You read the instructions carefully.

☐ C. You ask a friend to read them out to you.

**7.** You have vocabulary to learn for a test. How do you remember each word best?

☐ A. You see a picture of the word in your head.

☐ B. You practise writing it out several times.

☐ C. You say the word out loud.

**8.** Remember when you had to learn your tables? What helped most?

☐ A. Reciting them out loud.

☐ B. Seeing the brightly coloured table charts up in the classroom.

☐ C. Writing them out.

**9.** Which kind of lessons do you like the most?

☐ A. Lessons where there are lots of things to look at (for example geography – maps, charts, etc.).

☐ B. Lessons where there are lots of hands-on activity (for example CDT, science experiments).

☐ C. Lessons where you listen a lot (for example: history – listening to the teacher talk about battles, kings, queens, etc.).

**10.** You are at the supermarket, buying the equipment you need for your revision. How do you remember what to buy?

☐ A. You say the items to yourself, under your breath or in your head.

☐ B. You walk round the shelves, looking for the things that you need.

☐ C. You tick them off on the list that you have brought with you.

## Learning preferences

Put a ring round the letter that corresponds with your answer. For example, if your answer to question 1 is A put a ring round the V which is in the A column. Then add up your scores for each situation – how many Vs, As and Ks have you scored?

| Question | Answer A | Answer B | Answer C |
|:---:|:---:|:---:|:---:|
| 1 | V | K | A |
| 2 | A | V | K |
| 3 | A | K | V |
| 4 | V | A | K |
| 5 | K | A | V |
| 6 | K | V | A |
| 7 | V | K | A |
| 8 | A | V | K |
| 9 | V | K | A |
| 10 | A | V | K |

Totals
V ................    A ................    K ................

**Mostly Vs:** you are mainly a visual learner
(you like to learn by looking)

**Mostly As:** you are mainly an auditory learner
(you like to learn by listening)

**Mostly Ks:** you are mainly a kinaesthetic learner
(you like to learn by doing)

An even set of scores: you like all three ways of learning.

Here are the learning tips that work well for each learning preference. Start with the tips that match the way you like to learn best. Read these tips and write down the new learning techniques you promise to try out in the **I promise** box.

## Visual tips

- Use highlighter pens to make important words stand out when you are reading your notes or handouts.
- Use different coloured pens for writing out key points for revision.
- Use coloured sticky strips in your textbooks so you know where the important facts are.
- Use MIND MAPS® learning charts. Information is grouped by colour. You will learn more about learning charts in section 4.1
- Use coloured index cards. Have a different colour for each subject. If your school has a special colour for each subject, then match your system with your school's. If not, then make up a colour code of your own. You will learn more about how to use index cards in Section 4.3
- Use white index cards and still have a colour code for each subject. For example, put a yellow dot at the top of each history card, a blue dot for science and so on.
- Use notepads which are spiral bound. Start on the first left-hand page so you can use a double page at a time. Turn your notes into questions on the left-hand page and answers on the right-hand page. Use coloured pens for your notes and pictures.
- A really good time to check a MIND MAPS® learning chart, a set of cards or some double entry notes is just before you go to sleep. Remember, your brain will carry on learning the information for you as you go to sleep. A pretty good deal and one to make the most of!

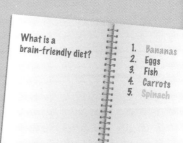

What is a brain-friendly diet?
1. Bananas
2. Eggs
3. Fish
4. Carrots
5. Spinach

### I promise

Which visual technique will you try out? Choose one. .................................

...................................................................................

## Auditory tips

- **Record your notes** on to a cassette and listen to your voice on the cassette. You will have lots of chances to make the most of your recordings. What about listening to them when you are in the car going to school?
- Get someone to **test you**.

- **Teach someone else** what you have just been learning about. Find someone who is willing to be your pupil – a grandparent, a parent or a friend.
- Read your notes **out loud** and make the most of your own voice.
- Use rhymes, raps and mnemonics, also known as **memory tricks**. You will learn more about memory tricks in Section 4.5
- Make up a **story** that links together all the key points that you are learning about.
- You can use MIND MAPS® learning charts. You should talk through the information on them. Linking a colourful learning chart with the sound of your voice is great for smart learning. You will learn more about these in Section 4.1

- You can use **spiral-bound notepads**. Start on the first left-hand page. Turn your notes into questions on the left-hand page and answers on the right-hand page. This method makes it easy to test yourself.
- **Talk through** your notes or **listen** to your cassettes just before you go to sleep. Remember, your brain will carry on learning the information for you whilst you go to sleep. A pretty good deal and one to make the most of!

I promise

Which auditory technique will you try out? Choose one. ....................................

..............................................................................................................................

- Kinaesthetic tips
  - **Walk up and down** as you read your notes. You are likely to be the fidget in the class so walking up and down keeps your body calm and helps your brain stay focused.
  - Give yourself **regular physical breaks** every 20 minutes. Do some stretches, move around or juggle for about five minutes and then start working again.

  - Use **sticky notes** for learning foreign language vocabulary. Write the English word on one sticky note and the foreign word on another. Put one sticky note on top of the other and test yourself. Tick each time you remember the word on the bottom sticky note. Then swap the sticky notes round and test yourself the other way round. What about using pink ones for feminine nouns and blue ones for masculine? Enjoy crumpling them up and putting them in the bin when you know the facts on them.
  - You can use MIND MAPS® **learning charts**. You will enjoy the activity of actually creating one. You will learn more about these in Section 4.1

- **Index cards** are really good for you. Test yourself with the cards in order, shuffle them, test yourself again and see if you can still remember the information. You will learn more about these in Section 4.3
- Use notepads to test yourself actively by writing out key points.
- Use everyday objects to make a model of what you are learning about. For example, you could make a 3D model of a volcano for geography with card, paint, pipe cleaners and glue.
- Play-acting and mime help make the facts you are learning about come alive. You could pretend to be a king or queen you are studying in history.
- Ask your parents to take you to the place you are learning about. This might be a museum, an exhibition, an office, an information centre, a river or many, many other locations.
- A really good time to check a set of your cards or sticky notes is just before you go to sleep. Remember, your brain will carry on learning the information for you as you go to sleep. A pretty good deal and one to make the most of!

I promise

Which kinaesthetic technique will you try out? Choose one...........................

......................................................................................................................

Keep these promises and you will be making the most of your learning preferences when you revise.

## Exercise 1.5: Extra tips
Which tips did you choose?

Visual ☐          Auditory ☐          Kinaesthetic ☐

Your next task is to read the tips that you skipped because you do not like learning this way. Check these out too and become an even smarter learner. Choose at least one more learning technique to try out.

I promise

Which extra learning technique/s will you try out? Choose at least one.

......................................................................................................................

......................................................................................................................

This is a really big step to take on your way to being a smart learner. Well done!

## Take a break

You have made some really important promises. Spend several days making them come true before you carry on reading.

## How smart are you becoming?

Give yourself a grade and only carry on reading when you are happy with your score.

- I use visual techniques

  A all the time ☐   B most of the time ☐   C some of the time ☐   D never ☐

- I use auditory techniques

  A all the time ☐   B most of the time ☐   C some of the time ☐   D never ☐

- I use kinaesthetic techniques

  A all the time ☐   B most of the time ☐   C some of the time ☐   D never ☐

Aim for A or B in your favourite learning technique. Aim for Bs or Cs in the others.  Now read on!

## Summary: Learn how you learn

Check out what you have learnt in the last section. Fill in the gaps to complete the key points.

### Smart learners know about their three main learning channels

- A visual learner likes to learn by looking
- My visual score was ...........
- An auditory learner likes to learn by listening
- My auditory score was ................
- A kinaesthetic learner likes to learn by doing
- My kinaesthetic score was ................

### Smart learners use techniques for all three learning preferences

- Visual learners use            **colour**
- Auditory learners use          **sound**
- Kinaesthetic learners use      **action**

# 1.3 Get the best from your memory

**1.** How many times have you blinked since starting to read this book?

**2.** How many steps did you take when you last went from the kitchen to your bedroom?

Surprise, surprise, you don't know the answers. Your brain works like a filter, making sure that you don't clutter it up with a lot of useless information. Unfortunately, facts that you really need to know get filtered out as well.

Read on and find out how to prevent this from happening.

## Beat the memory dip

You remember best at the beginning and at the end of a learning session. Your memory powers dip in the middle of that time.

This is what the memory dip looks like on a graph.

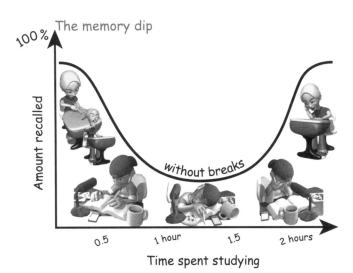

Beat the memory dip

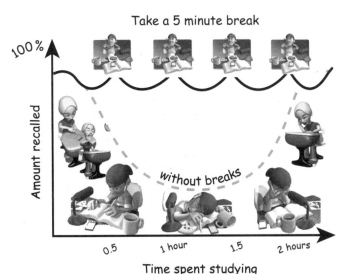

You can beat the memory dip by giving yourself lots of beginnings and endings in your study time by taking short breaks. Learn for 20–30 minutes then take a break.

### All about breaks

Breaks during a learning session must be short: about five minutes long. There are many activities that are good for a short break. Here are a few:

- Listen to your favourite music. This puts you in a positive mood.
- Eat a brain-friendly snack.
- Have a drink of water. This helps to activate the brain.
- Get some exercise. This helps send more oxygen to the brain.
- Juggle. This gets both hemispheres of the brain working well together and is also an oxygen booster.

Make sure you get back to work after five minutes. Set an alarm to go off – you probably have one on your watch or ask a friend to tell you when your time is up.

After your break, spend two or three minutes reviewing (checking over) what you learned before. This will really help get those facts into your memory before you move on to something new.

### Watch out!

Don't cheat on yourself! Here are some of the bad things to do in a break.

1. Read a book.
2. Play on the computer.
3. Watch television.
4. Phone a friend for a chat.

Here are the reasons why they are bad:
- New information coming in will clash with what your brain is still trying to learn.
- When did you last do any of these activities for just five minutes? Remember, these breaks must be short.

This doesn't mean that you cannot watch TV at all. It just means that you should save TV, computer games and chatting to friends until the very end of your study time. Give yourself some treats to look forward to. Treats help to keep you thinking positively too. This may mean some radical changes to your work habits but it will be worth it.

## Beat the memory slide

Here is another problem your memory faces. It is possible to forget up to 80% of what you have learnt after only 24 hours. Your knowledge simply disappears down the memory slide.

This is what the memory slide looks like on a graph.

Read on and find out how to prevent this from happening.

You can fix new facts in your memory by reviewing (checking over) what you have learned. If you review these facts at regular intervals, you will send them into your long-term memory. This is the brain's storage depot for knowledge it will not forget. Once facts are there, you will find it much, much easier to remember what you need to know in tests and exams. The next exercise will show you how to do this.

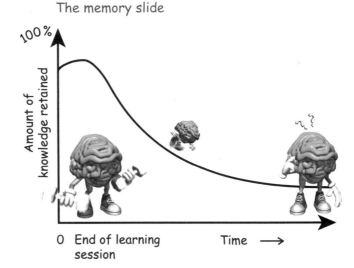

The memory slide

## Exercise 1.6: The reviewing routine

Use the following method for any facts your brain finds really difficult to learn. Let's call them tough facts. These might be French, German or Latin vocabulary, history dates, maths or science formulae. Which are tough facts for you?

My tough facts are ...................................................................................................

The great news is that you can become expert at tough facts if you review them regularly so that your brain gets to know them really well.

Regular reviewing should take place at the following times:
• five minutes later
• one day later
• one week later
• one month later

You will need the following equipment:
• A numbered concertina file. There will be 31 sections in your file, numbered from 1 to 31, the same as the number of days in most months.
• Small blank playing cards or index cards.
• Pens

Now follow the **step-by-step** guide to mastery of tough facts.

**Step 1:** Choose a set of tough facts that you need to learn. Break your learning into manageable chunks. For foreign vocabulary, aim for between five and ten words in one session.

**Step 2:** Write them on your cards. For example, if you have chosen foreign vocabulary, write the English on one side of the card and the foreign word on the other. Whenever possible, use both sides of your cards as this makes it easier to test yourself.

**Step 3:** **Look (visual)** at your cards, **say** the facts **out loud (auditory)** and **write** them out **(kinaesthetic)**. Put your cards in two piles: one for the facts you know and one for the ones you don't. Have another go at learning the ones in the second pile. Keep adding the facts that you know to the first pile and testing yourself on the ones that you don't. This stage could last for up to 20 minutes.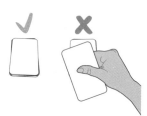

**Step 4:** Take a five minute break. Remember the good things to do during your break (see page 20).

**Step 5:** Spend a few minutes testing yourself again. This is your **five minute review**.

**Step 6:** Put your cards into the correct section of your numbered concertina file. To do this you need to find out what the date is, add on one and put them in the numbered section that matches this number.

**Step 7:** The next day, remove the cards from your file and test yourself again. This is your **one day review**.

**Step 8:** Count on seven and put your cards in their new place in your concertina file. Check your file every day: just the section that matches the date that day.

**Step 9:** One week later, test yourself again. This is your **one week review**.

**Step 10:** Write the name of next month at the top of your cards and put them back in the same place in your file.

**Step 11:** One month later, test yourself. This is your **one month review**.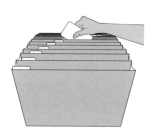

**Step 12:** When reviewing is finished, store your cards in an index box. You may well want to check them all again just before a test or exam.

Look at the next graph and see how much more knowledge you keep in your brain when you use the reviewing routine.

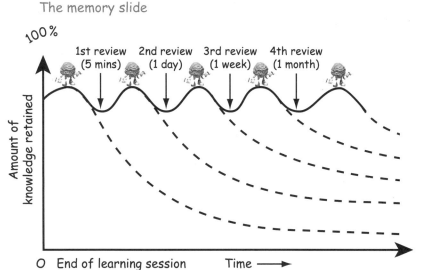

The memory slide

100%

1st review (5 mins)  2nd review (1 day)  3rd review (1 week)  4th review (1 month)

Amount of knowledge retained

O   End of learning session     Time ⟶

## Tips for reviewing

- You are likely to need someone in your family to help you stick to your routine.
- Get into the habit of checking your file at the same time every day. What about just before you go to bed so your brain can carry on reviewing whilst you go to sleep?
- Remember, test yourself on the cards in the section that matches the day's date.

## I promise

How are you going to beat the memory dip?

**1.** I shall work for ……………………. minutes before I take a short break.

**2.** During my short break I shall ………………………………………………………………
………………………………………………………………………………………………

**3.** I shall review what I have just been learning before I start a new topic.

How are you going to beat the memory slide?

**4.** I shall use the reviewing routine for the following tough facts …………………….
………………………………………………………………………………………………

**5.** I shall ask ………………………………. to help me stick to my routine.

### Take a break

You have made some more very important promises. Spend several days making them come true before you carry on reading.

### Are you making the most of your memory?

Give yourself a grade and carry on reading when you are happy with your score.

- I work for 20-30 minutes, take a short break, then review what I have just been learning:

  A all the time ☐     B most of the time ☐     C some of the time ☐     D never ☐

- I use the reviewing routine to help me learn tough facts:

  A all the time ☐     B most of the time ☐     C some of the time ☐     D never ☐

# Summary: Get the best from your memory

## Beat the memory dip with a good learning routine

- Revise for 20-30 minutes.
- Take a five minute break.
- Choose a good activity for a short break such as juggling, eating a brain-friendly snack, having a drink of water, listening to your favourite music.
- Spend a few minutes reviewing what you have just learnt.
- Start a new topic and repeat the same routine.

## Beat the memory slide with a regular reviewing routine

- Regular reviewing for tough facts will get them fixed into your long-term memory.
- Review these facts five minutes later, one day later, one week later and one month later.
- Use a numbered concertina file for regular reviewing.
- A good time to check your file is just before you go to sleep.

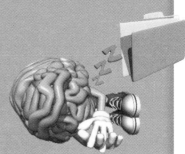

# 2 Are you ready?

## 2.1 Getting motivated

Thanks to all those promises you have made in Chapter 1, you should now be well on the way to becoming a smart learner. But what if you cannot be bothered to keep your promises? This is a problem most students face from time to time.

You have to want to learn. When you want something, this motivates you to find a way to get it. Imagine you want to buy a new game for your computer. Perhaps you save your pocket money. Perhaps you earn extra money by washing your parents' car. Soon you are off to the shops to buy that game. Goal achieved! How do you feel when you load it into your computer? You feel great.

Achieving goals makes us feel good. It is the same with tests and exams. If you do as well as you can, you will feel great. So give your learning a purpose by setting yourself goals that matter to you and that you know you can achieve.

### Exercise 2.1: Set yourself goals

**1. What?**

　(a) Write down the subjects you are good at: ......................................................

　　.............................................................................................................

　　.............................................................................................................

　(b) What grades are you aiming for in these subjects?.......................................

　　.............................................................................................................

　　.............................................................................................................

　(c) Write down the subjects which you could be good at if you worked harder: .......

　　.............................................................................................................

　　.............................................................................................................

　(d) What grades are you aiming for in these subjects?.......................................

　　.............................................................................................................

　　.............................................................................................................

　(e) Are there any subjects you really struggle with? If there are, write these down:

　　.............................................................................................................

　　.............................................................................................................

(f) What grades are you aiming for in these subjects?......................................

...............................................................................................................

...............................................................................................................

## 2. When?

You must decide when you need to achieve these goals by. Is it in time for a test or for school examintions? You must choose.

I aim to achieve my goals by..............................................................................

...............................................................................................................

## 3. Why?

Why do your goals matter to you? Think hard about this and choose the reasons that are really important to you. Is it because you will feel great when you are successful? Is it because your next school is a fantastic place to aim for? If so, why?

My goals are important to me because ..............................................................

...............................................................................................................

### Tips about goals

- You have more chance of achieving your goals if you write them down. The goals you have just set yourself are the first step to success.
- You may need new goals from time to time. Just write them out using the format above.
- How about pinning them up next to your desk to remind you what you are aiming for?

# 2.2 Your back-up team

So now you've decided on your goals. Well done. Luckily you are not expected to achieve them all on your own. You are the team leader and you have a back-up team to help you.

Top athletes preparing for a big competition know how to get the best out of their back-up team to help them improve their performance. They will have a coach, a physiotherapist, a dietician, a sport psychologist and a manager.

So who is in your back-up team? And what can they do to help you?

● Your teachers
- Teachers give you the big picture of what you need to learn. They usually give out revision lists so you know what to revise. Make sure you keep these at the front of your subject files.
- They give you the detail you need. If you don't understand a teaching point, be smart and ask your teacher for help.
- They have a supply of textbooks and handouts. If you have lost your notes, make sure you ask for some extra handouts.
- Teachers are the exam experts. If you're not sure what to expect, ask your teacher to explain. Ask for a practice paper to try out.

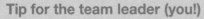

**Tip for the team leader (you!)**
Really work on your relationship with your teachers. If you show them you want to succeed, they will want to help you.

## Your family

Ask your family to make sure:
- you get brain-friendly food; and
- you have all the vital equipment you need.

Ask your family to help:
- test you and be good listeners when you explain a topic to them; and
- keep you on track with your routine.

Ask your family to give you those really important treats you are going to reward yourself with for working so hard!

**Tip for the team leader (you!)**
Really work on your relationship with the family members in your team. Do your parents often nag you about your work? Stop this from happening by showing them what a smart learner you are. Tell them when you plan to do your work. Ask them when they can test you. They will be so impressed, they will not want to nag you any more.

## Your friends

Friends are very important. They will:
- chat things through with you;
- keep you cheerful;
- help out with lost notes; and
- go out with you on those very important days off.

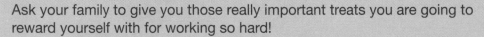

**Tip for the team leader (you!)**
Really work at choosing friends who have goals they care about too.

Avoid the 'Couldn't-Care-Less' crowd. They will only hold you back.

Keep up with your out-of-school friends. They are great for meeting up with for a complete break from work.

# 2.3 Getting organised

Getting organised before you start to revise really pays off. Here are three ways to get yourself ready for revision.

## Where should you work?

It's a top priority to have your own workspace. Where will this be? A desk in your bedroom is fine. If not, make sure you use a quiet room where you can leave your books between revision sessions.

So, now you've got your workspace sorted out, what state is it in? Does it need tidying up? Well, get on with it! Clear away anything you don't need.

- Tips for where you work
  - Make sure your desk is well lit.
  - Your room should be warm, but not stuffy (18–23 °C).
  - Your seat should give you good support and be at a height where you can easily rest your non-writing arm on the desk.

## What equipment do you need?

Once you have your workspace sorted out, ask yourself whether you have everything you need. Here is an equipment checklist. Use this to make sure you are stocked up with all those extra bits of equipment that will help with your smart learning.

| | | | |
|---|---|---|---|
| Fine liners (coloured) | ☐ | Index box | ☐ |
| Felt tips (thin/thick) | ☐ | Subject dividers (for index box and ring binders) | ☐ |
| Gel pens | ☐ | Spiral-bound notepads to open sideways | ☐ |
| Highlighters | ☐ | A3 plain paper for MIND MAPS®learning charts | ☐ |
| Sticky notes | ☐ | A3 plastic envelopes to store learning charts | ☐ |
| Numbered concertina file | ☐ | Blank playing cards* and a box to store them in | ☐ |
| Index cards: coloured/ white | ☐ | Cassettes and a box to store them in | ☐ |

*See the 'Resources' section on page 80 for availability

## Tips for while you work
- Have some drinking water available.
- Do you like to listen to music whilst you work?

**If yes:**
Some researchers believe right-brain thinkers like music in the background. It keeps their right hemisphere happy and helps them concentrate on all those left-brain lists of facts they need to learn. Baroque music is great for this. Bach (Brandenburg Concertos), Handel (Water Music) and Vivaldi (Four Seasons) are just a few examples of suitable music. Environmental music is great too. Ocean sounds, waterfalls and rain forest soundtracks work well in the background.

**If no:**
That's fine. Left-brain thinkers are likely to prefer complete quiet. Experiment and find out what works best for you.

## Watch out!
Do not listen to pop music or the radio while you are learning. Why are your favourite pop tunes bad for learning? Because the words in the pop songs will clash with the facts you are learning. Save your favourite music for your breaks.

## When should you work?
Here are some practical suggestions to help you decide when you are going to revise.

## Term time
Set aside 30 minutes in the evening for one topic. This means 20 minutes active learning, a five minute break and three to five minutes checking what you have just learnt.

Remember, you can always record The Simpsons! Think how much you can boost your exam grades just by recording one TV programme a night. What about giving yourself a weekend treat with a bumper viewing of your favourite weekday programme?

## Weekends/holidays
What time of day is best for you? Be honest. Be consistent. It's much easier to work when you have a routine you are used to. What about a 30 minute slot after breakfast? If the exams are getting close, extend this to two, even three slots.

The good news is that, the better organised you are, the more time you will have for fun activities. Choose some treats to look forward to and remember your goals. The important thing is to get started. It is going to feel good when your grades start climbing.

● Work planners

You can download both the year and weekly planners from the Galore Park website www.galorepark.co.uk. These will help you organise your time. You can also download topic and subject checklists. These will help you keep on top of what you are revising. Choose one kind of planner to try out first and get into the habit of making good use of it. Follow the step-by-step guide to planners in the next exercise so you get the best out of them. A good one to start with is the year planner.

## Exercise 2.2: Using work planners

**1. Using a year planner** ( www.galorepark.co.uk )

(a) Download a copy of the year planner from the Galore Park website at www. galorepark.co.uk.

(b) Fill in the items below using a different colour for each one. Start with the fun things! Notice just how much holiday you have and think of all those treats you will have plenty of time for when your studying is over.

  • Your birthday          • School holidays

Now fill in your study commitments.

  • The dates of exams          • The dates when projects are due in

(c) Pin your planner up. Make sure you check it regularly so that you allow enough time to revise for exams and to complete your projects.

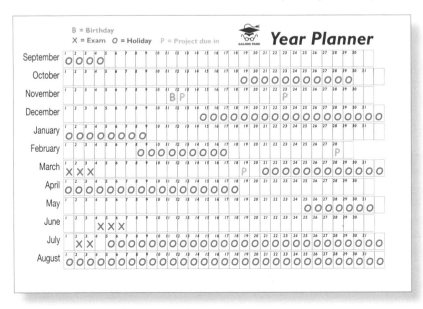

## 2. Using a weekly planner (www.galorepark.co.uk)

(a) Download as many copies of the weekly planner as you need from the Galore Park website. If you start revising two weeks before the exams, you will need two weekly planners.

(b) Fill in the fun things first by choosing your day off! You need to reward yourself for all that smart learning with some fun as well.

(c) Choose which subjects you are going to revise and when. Fill these in on your weekly planner, making sure to choose the time of day that is best for you.

(d) Pin your planner up and make sure you check it every day.

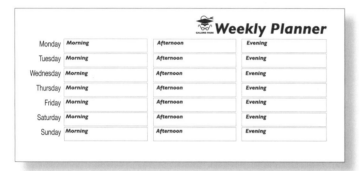

## 3. Using a topic checklist (www.galorepark.co.uk)

(a) Download as many copies of the topic checklist as you need from the Galore Park website. You need one per subject.

(b) Write the name of the subject at the top.

(c) Write down the topics that you need to revise for that particular subject. Use a number code to make it clear what order you should revise your topics in:

    1. vital       2. important       3. if you have time

You may need help from your teacher to sort your topics into these categories.

(d) Keep your topic checklist at the front of your subject file, if you have one. If not, keep all your topic checklists in a special file for revision. Check them regularly.

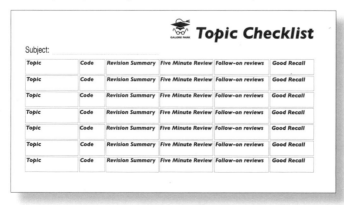

## 4. Using a subject checklist  ( www.galorepark.co.uk )

(a) Download a copy of the subject checklist from the Galore Park website.

(b) Tick every time that you revise a subject. This is an easy, at-a-glance way of seeing that you are keeping on top of all your subjects. Of course, you may not be studying all of the subjects on this checklist.

(c) Pin your planner up next to your weekly planner and check it regularly. Are you keeping to your schedule? If not, how do you need to change it?

### 🎓 Subject Checklist

| | |
|---|---|
| English | |
| Maths | |
| Science<br>* Life and living processes<br><br>* Materials and their properties<br><br>* Physical proceses | |
| History | |
| Geography | |
| Religious Studies | |
| Latin | |
| Greek | |
| French | |

### I promise

How are you going to become a great team leader?

**1.** I shall write down my goals:    Every term ☐  Every month ☐

**2.** I shall make the most of the following people in my back-up team ..................

.........................................................................................................................

**3.** I shall improve my workspace by .........................................................

.........................................................................................................................

**4.** I shall buy the following equipment .......................................................

.........................................................................................................................

**5.** I shall use work planners. I shall try out a .............................. planner first.

**Take a break**
You have made some more very important promises. Spend several days making them come true before you carry on reading.

Are you becoming a great team leader?
Give yourself a grade and carry on reading when you are happy with your score.

• I am a great team leader:

A all the time ☐     B most of the time ☐     C some of the time ☐     D never ☐

# Summary: Are you ready?

### Smart learners set themselves goals
• They know what they want to achieve.
• They know how long they need.
• They know why their goals matter.

### Smart learners make the most of their back-up team
• They make the most of their teachers.
• They make the most of their family.
• They make the most of their friends.

### Smart learners get organised
• They have a tidy workspace.
• They have all the equipment they need.
• They use work planners to keep them on track.

Smart learners are great team leaders because they get themselves organised and they have more time for fun.

# 3 Active learning

Thanks to all those promises you made in Chapter 2, you are ready to learn. But what if you just sit at your tidy, well-equipped desk letting all those facts you are reading about go drifting in and out of your brain? What a waste of your time! You need to become expert at making your learning active.

There are many ways to keep your brain alert and learning actively but here are three basic skills you need a bit of extra training in first. You should use them when you are learning any topic that requires a lot of reading. You also need them for the revision techniques you will learn about in Chapter 4.

## 3.1 Brain warm-ups

Brain warm-ups are just like warm-ups for sport. They get your brain ready to revise.

Give your brain a warm-up by asking yourself this question about any topic that you are about to revise:

### What do I already know about this topic?
- Spend two or three minutes jotting down absolutely anything that you can think of to do with your revision topic. Left-brain thinkers may want to do this as a list.
- Right-brain thinkers may prefer having a bubble in the centre of the page and drawing lines out from the centre. Only write single words or phrases.
- Jot ideas down as they pop into your head. Order does not matter at this stage. This is called brainstorming.
- After the brain warm-up there is another really important question to ask yourself:

Mount Etna
Lava and Ash　Erupt

### What else do I need to know about this topic?
- Now get started on that vital reading of your notes. I will show you ways to do this in Sections 3.2 and 3.3 so that you keep all those important facts inside your brain.

Exercise 3.1: Brain warm-ups

I will use a geography topic – volcanoes – to help you become expert in the three active learning skills. This should be a topic that you know a little about, even if you have not yet studied it at school. Spend two or three minutes writing down anything you already know about volcanoes below:

Either jot down your ideas in a list or in a circle round the central bubble.

Brain warm-up

What do I already know about volcanoes? Either write your thoughts down as a list:

1. ................................................................................................................................

2. ................................................................................................................................

3. ................................................................................................................................

4. ................................................................................................................................

5. ................................................................................................................................

6. ................................................................................................................................

Or write your thoughts in a circle around this central bubble:

Volcanoes

---

● Tips about brain warm-ups

- A brain warm-up is like putting hooks in your head. More of what you read will hang on your hooks.
- Keep your warm-ups on file. Do another brainstorm after revising a topic. You will feel good when you see how much more you know.
- You have found out what you already know so your brain can now focus on learning new stuff. This is a great way of helping you make the best use of your time.

# 3.2 Key words

Your brain is now fantastically warmed-up and ready to learn. Here is your next important question:

What else do I need to know about volcanoes?

To answer this question you will need to read the passage about volcanoes below. However, there is another vital skill you need – the ability to pick out key words when you have a lot of notes to read.

Key words are the main information words in your reading material. Your brain works like a sieve, filtering out the little words and keeping all those important fact-filled words there.

## Volcanoes

Volcanoes are openings in the Earth's surface which allow magma, ash and gas to escape from deep below the Earth's surface. When volcanoes erupt, the magma from below the earth's surface rises up the vent to the volcano's crater. It then explodes into the air as ash, dust and volcanic bombs or flows out as molten lava.

An active volcano is a volcano which has recently erupted or is likely to erupt again. There are over 700 in the world today. A dormant volcano is a volcano which has erupted in the past 2000 years, but not recently. These types of volcanoes are dangerous as it is difficult to predict when they might erupt again. Finally, an extinct volcano is unlikely to erupt again.

The earth's crust is formed by several enormous sections called plates. They move on a layer of molten rock (the mantle) a few millimetres a year. The plate boundary is where the plates meet. Volcanoes are limited to certain areas or belts along plate boundaries where two plates meet. One belt runs all the way round the edge of the Pacific Ocean and is called 'The Ring of Fire'.

Mount Etna is the largest active volcano in Europe. Thousands of people live on its slopes because the volcanic soil is very fertile. Farmers are able to grow high yields of crops such as grapes, oranges and olives. In 2002–2003 the eruptions threw up a huge column of ash that could be seen from space.

## Exercise 3.2: Key words

Start with the first paragraph of the volcanoes passage. Have a go at underlining the key words. Do not underline too much. You may prefer to use highlighters. Be careful. Do not highlight too much. You do not want to end up with a passage that looks so colourful you can't pick out the key words any more.

Here's how to do it using the first sentence.

Volcanoes are <u>openings</u> in the <u>Earth's surface</u> which allow <u>magma</u>, <u>ash</u> and <u>gas</u> to <u>escape</u> from <u>deep below</u> the <u>Earth's surface</u>.

### Key word coding

Can you crack the code? Look at the following sentence from the volcanoes passage. See if you can work out why certain words are now being underlined in different ways.

One | <u>belt</u> runs all the way round the <u>edge</u> of the <u>Pacific Ocean</u> and is called 'The Ring of Fire'.

Code

| Important words | <u>belt</u> |
|---|---|
| Names | Pacific Ocean |
| Numbers | one |

### Exercise 3.3: Key word coding

Try this out with the rest of the volcanoes passage on page 37. When you use the key word code, it is better to use a fineliner or a pencil rather than a highlighter.

# 3.3 Making notes

This skill is vital for your revision summaries. You need to be good at summing up the main points of your topic. Making notes is active. Your brain works like a sieve, saving all the key points and getting rid of the little words.

Do you have a mobile phone? If you do, then here is a great opportunity for you to make the most of your text messaging skills!

### Watch out!

Have you ever found that when you make revision summaries you end up rewriting your class notes? This is just copying. Your brain can have a nice nap while you just copy out your work in smaller handwriting. Don't waste your time doing this. You will find it easier and quicker to make notes if you learn a set of useful abbreviations first. Here are some for you to choose from.

## General abbreviations

| | | | |
|---|---|---|---|
| and | & | and so on | etc |
| because | b/c | as soon as possible | asap |
| therefore | ∴ | important | imp |
| for example | eg | through | thro' |
| that is to say | ie | including | incl |
| take note/note well | NB | possible | poss |

## A selection of subject abbreviations

| | | | |
|---|---|---|---|
| introduction | intro | North | N |
| conclusion | concl | South | S |
| character | char | maximum | max |
| century | C | minimum | min |
| 16th century | ⑯ | number | no |
| government | gov | equal | = |
| parliament | parl | greater than | > |
| Battle of | ⚔ | less than | < |
| versus | vs | year | yr |
| Edward III * | E III | hour | hr |
| Old Testament | O. Test | minute | min |
| New Testament | N. Test | millimetre | mm |

*Use intials for battles, kings and queens

● Tips for using abbreviations
  • Be creative. Make up some of your own.
  • Be consistent. Use the same abbreviation for the same word each time.
  • It is sometimes better to write difficult words out in full so you get used to spelling them correctly.

Exercise 3.4: Making notes

**1.** Practise making notes from the following statements. Two are taken from the volcanoes passage you have already read, one from the William the Conqueror passage on page 50 and one from the life processes passage on page 55.

(a) Volcanoes are openings in the Earth's surface which allow magma, ash and gas to escape from deep below the Earth's surface.

.........................................................................................................................................

(b) One belt runs all the way round the edge of the Pacific Ocean and is called 'The Ring of Fire'.

.........................................................................................................................................

(c) The winds changed in late September when Harold was in the north fighting the king of Norway, Harald Hardrada and Tostig at Stamford Bridge.

.........................................................................................................................................

(d) Movement in animals means moving from place to place to find food. In plants it means moving towards a stimulus.

.........................................................................................................................................

**Answers:**
(a) Volcanoes = openings in ground. Magma, ash, dust ➜ earth's surface.
(b) 1 belt round edge Pacific Ocean: Ring of Fire.
(c) Winds changed late Sept. Harold in N. ✕ SB vs K. Norway, Harald Hardrada[*]
    & Tostig.
(d) Animals move place 2 place ➜ food. Plants move ➜ stimulus.

[*]Notice I kept Harald Hardrada's name in full. It is difficult to spell so I wanted extra practice.

**2.** You need to be able to read your notes easily and know exactly what key points you made. So let's check how good your notes are. Finish this exercise a day later.

**A day later**
Go back to your practice notes. Cover up the statements above them. Can you turn your notes back into full sentences?

(a) .....................................................................................................................................

.........................................................................................................................................

(b) ..................................................................................................................

..................................................................................................................

(c) ..................................................................................................................

..................................................................................................................

(d) ..................................................................................................................

..................................................................................................................

## Watch out!

If you can't understand your own notes, it probably means you have made them so short that they no longer make sense. Keep on practising until you know you have the balance right.

### I promise

**1.** Which topic will you try your first brain warm-up with? ......................................

**2.** Will you use a fineliner, pencil or a highlighter to make key words stand out?

..................................................................................................................

**3.** Which abbreviations will you learn off by heart so you can use them easily in your revision notes? Practise them here:

| Full | Abreviation | Full | Abreviation |
|------|-------------|------|-------------|
|      |             |      |             |
|      |             |      |             |
|      |             |      |             |
|      |             |      |             |
|      |             |      |             |

Keep these promises and you are even further along the way to being a smart learner.

### Take a break

You have made some more very important promises. Spend several days making them come true before you carry on reading.

Are you making your learning active?

Give yourself a grade and carry on reading when you are happy with your score.

• I learn actively.

A all the time ☐     B most of the time ☐     C some of the time ☐     D never ☐

## Summary: Active learning

Smart learners make sure they learn actively

• They start with a brain warm-up:
  They ask the question: What do I already know about my topic?
  They follow this with another question: What else do I need to know?

• They make key words stand out:
  They underline or highlight the fact-filled words.
  They know how to use a key word code.

• They know how to make good notes:
  They use abbreviations.
  They can turn their notes back into full statements.

Smart learners make the best possible use of the time they spend learning.

# 4 Amazing revision techniques

How do you like to learn? Are you a step-by-step left-brain thinker or a big picture right-brain thinker? Which of your visual, auditory and kinaesthetic strengths do you like using? Which new strengths do you want to develop? It is important that you know. Look back at Chapter 1 to remind yourself.

You are now going to find out about four revision techniques and a stack of other handy tips. Thanks to your new understanding of how you learn you will be able to choose the techniques that really work for you. This is smart learning at its best.

## 4.1 MIND MAPS® learning charts

Pioneered by Tony Buzan, MIND MAPS® learning charts is a technique that uses colour, pictures, key words, grouping and FUN to help you remember. Right-brain thinkers will enjoy seeing a whole topic summed up on one sheet of paper with colour and pictures. Left-brain thinkers will enjoy adding all the extra detail in a clearly structured way. We will start by learning the basic technique. We will turn as many key points as possible into pictures. We will also use abbreviations in our notes. When you make MIND MAPS® learning charts for other topics, you can develop your own personal style.

### Equipment you will need
• A3 plain paper.
• A selection of good quality felt tip pens of different thicknesses.
• A3 plastic envelope for storage.

### Exercise 4.1: Creating a MIND MAPS® learning chart
We will continue with our geography topic – volcanoes. It does not matter if you have not studied this topic at school yet because you only need the information in the passage on page 37 for this first MIND MAPS® learning chart. Follow the steps below:

**Step 1: Brain warm-up**
What do I already know about volcanoes?
You have already completed this step. Look on
page 36 to remind yourself of what you already know.

**Step 2: Key words**
What else do I want to know about volcanoes?
Reread the passage about volcanoes on page 37. Check you have already
underlined/highlighted the key words.

**Step 3: Key words into pictures**
Practise turning some of these key words into pictures. You do not have to be a great
artist. Stick people and very simple drawings are fine. Funny drawings are great. Make
sure you use these pictures in your MIND MAPS® learning chart. Your brain will love
remembering them, especially if they are funny.

| | | | |
|---|---|---|---|
| volcano | | active | |
| magma | | dormant | |
| crater | | extinct | |
| ash | | plate boundary | |
| dust | | Ring of Fire | |
| volcanic bombs | | farmers | |
| lava | | grapes | |

## Step 4: Into action

- Place your A3 paper in a horizontal position on your desk. Keep it in this position the whole time, as though glued to the desk. If you twist the paper about, then you will end up writing some key words upside down and will not be able to learn easily from your MIND MAPS® learning chart.
- **Central image:** This is like a title. What is the passage about? Easy – VOLCANOES. Draw a picture in the centre of your sheet of paper to sum up your topic. Do not make it too big. If you don't want to draw a picture, then write your key word, VOLCANO in capital letters and enclose the word in an oval. This should be about the size of an egg.

- **First main branch:** Look at the key words in the first paragraph. Can you think of a question word that sums up the main idea in this paragraph? I suggest the question word WHAT? Look at your central image and choose a colour from it. Position your first branch at 2 o'clock. Draw two thick lines in this colour that curve outwards from the central image and end in a point. Fill your branch with a simple pattern, still in the same colour. Write the key word WHAT? along the top of your main branch in capital letters.
- **First set of sub-branches:** Look at the key words in the first paragraph again. What are the key points about volcanoes? How many are there? Draw single line branches starting at the end of the main branch. Draw one at a time for each key point. Use your pictures to sum up each key point. Any words should be printed in lower case. As my main branch is black, I use black for sub-branches, pictures and words. I am grouping information by colour as well as content. You can also use other colours in your pictures when you want them to look like the real thing.

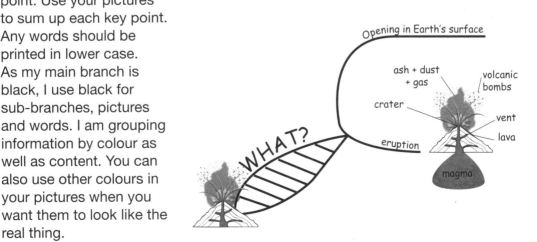

- **Second main branch:** Look at the key words in the second paragraph. Can you think of one word that sums up the main idea in this paragraph? I suggest TYPES. Choose a new colour. Draw your next branch at 4 o'clock. Write the key word TYPES along the top in capital letters.
- **Second set of sub-branches:** How many key points are there about the types of volcanoes? Draw your sub-branches, one at a time, and add pictures to sum up each key point. Add as many sub branches as you need. Remember to print any words you need in lower case.
- **Third main branch:** Look at the key words in the third paragraph. Can you think of one word that sums up the main idea in this paragraph? I suggest another question word: WHERE? Choose a new colour. Draw your next branch at 8 o'clock. Write the key word WHERE? along the top in capital letters.
- **Third set of sub-branches:** How many key points are there about where we find volcanoes? Draw your sub-branches, one at a time, and add pictures to sum up each key point.

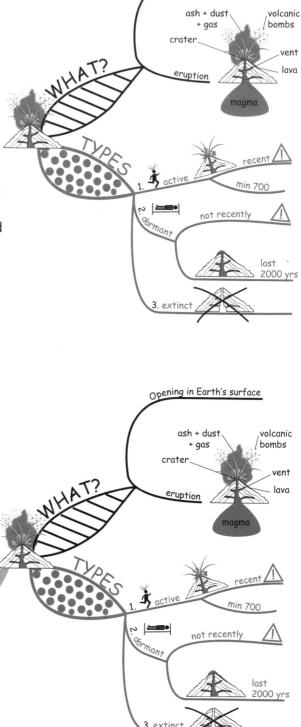

• **Fourth main branch:** What would you do? How about doing this one on your own? This is my finished MIND MAPS® learning chart.

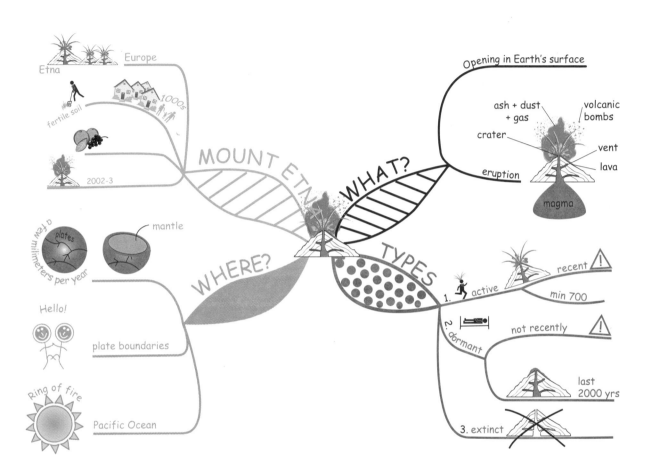

● Tips for making the most of the MIND MAPS® learning charts method
- Make your MIND MAPS® learning charts when your teacher finishes a topic.
- You can have more main branches – five or six is fine for a bigger topic. Just make sure you space them out well on your sheet of paper.
- You may prefer fewer pictures and more words. Experiment and find out what works best for you.
- Store your MIND MAPS® learning charts in A3 plastic envelopes. Have one envelope per subject.
- Before exams, put your MIND MAPS® learning charts up on the wall. Have all the maps for one particular subject in one place. Only leave them up whilst you are actively learning from them. Do not let them become a kind of revision wallpaper!
- Remember your learning routine. Learn for 20 minutes. Take a break. Review. Make the most of your learning strengths:
  - Visual learners: Picture your MIND MAPS® learning chart in your mind.
  - Auditory learners: Get a parent or friend to test you on it. Talk it through to yourself.
  - Kinaesthetic learners: Fill in the details on a blank MIND MAPS® learning chart.

---

I promise ✓

A good geography topic to try out on your own is the water cycle.

Which exam topic will you use for your first MIND MAPS® learning chart?

.......................................................................................................................

# 4.2 Box and bubble flow charts

This is another technique where right-brain thinkers will enjoy seeing a whole topic summed up on one page and left-brain thinkers will enjoy adding the extra detail in a clearly structured way. Flow charts are good for students who prefer to make their summaries in a vertical format. Key points are connected downwards and sideways by lines. They are surrounded by boxes or bubbles. We will focus on turning key points into brief notes.

## Equipment you will need
• A3 plain paper. You can use A4 if you prefer, but try A3 first.
• Fine liner pens, gel pens or felt tips in different colours.

## Exercise 4.2: Creating a box and bubble flow chart
We will use a history topic – Why William the Conqueror won the Battle of Hastings. It does not matter if you have not studied this topic at school because you only need the information in the passage on page 50 for this first flow chart. Follow the steps below.

**Step 1: Brain warm-up**
What do I already know about why William won the Battle of Hastings?

Jot down single words in a list or in a ring round the central bubble below. Just spend two or three minutes doing this.

Why William won the Battle of Hastings:
Either as a list:　　　　　　　　　　　　　　　Or in a circle round a bubble:

1. ...............................................
2. ...............................................
3. ...............................................
4. ...............................................
5. ...............................................

Why William won the Battle of Hastings

**Step 2: Key words**
What else do I want to know about why William won the Battle of Hastings?
Read the passage on the next page to find out more. Underline or highlight the key words. What about using the key word code? Check this out on page 38. Remember, you are making your reading as active as possible.

## Why William won the Battle of Hastings

There are several reasons why William of Normandy won the Battle of Hastings. Firstly, he was a very determined and ambitious leader. He claimed Harold had promised to help him become king. He gained the support of the Pope and marched into battle with the papal banner. This meant his army believed God was on their side. He made thorough preparations for the invasion through the spring and summer of 1066.

Secondly, William was lucky. He had been waiting all summer for favourable winds to carry his fleet to England. The winds changed in late September when Harold was in the north fighting the king of Norway, Harald Hardrada, and Tostig at Stamford Bridge. William landed his army near Pevensey on a completely undefended coast on 28th September 1066.

Thirdly, Harold's army was exhausted. They had just fought and won the Battle of Stamford Bridge. Harold marched south to face William as quickly as he could, covering 180 miles in four days. Many of his best fighters, the housecarls, were killed or wounded. He left many of his archers behind. His men were all on foot. Many of them were untrained farmers known as the Fyrd. They were brave but not very well disciplined. They locked shields during the Battle of Hastings to form a shield wall which was very difficult to break.

Finally, William had a strong and disciplined army made up of archers, infantry and cavalry. William planned a series of fake retreats. These tricked the untrained Fyrd. They left the safety of the hill and ran after the Normans who cut them down at the bottom of the hill. The shield wall was broken, Harold was killed and the Saxons fled. After a whole day of fierce fighting, William won the battle and became the king of England when he was crowned on Christmas Day in 1066.

**Step 3: Topic abbreviations**
Practise turning some of these words into abbreviations and then use them in your flow chart.

| | | | |
|---|---|---|---|
| William of Normandy | | Harold | |
| Battle of Hastings | | Stamford Bridge | |
| preparations | | England | |
| September | | Christmas | |

**Step 4: Into action**
- Place your paper in a vertical position on your desk.

- Title. What is this passage about? Write your title at the top of the page in capital letters. I suggest WHY WILLIAM WON THE BATTLE OF HASTINGS.

- **First paragraph**: Look at the key words in the first paragraph. Can you think of one word or phrase that sums up the main idea in this paragraph? I suggest WILLIAM. Start at the top of the page. Write this word in capitals and surround it with a box. Draw lines out to the right and make notes on each point about William. Use lower case letters for your notes. Surround each set of notes in a bubble. Link the bubbles with lines. Here's how.

- **Second paragraph**: Look at the key words in the second paragraph. Can you think of one word or phrase that sums up the main idea in this paragraph? I suggest WILLIAM'S LUCK. Draw a line down from your WILLIAM box to connect it with your second box. Now add your notes out to the side in the same way as before.

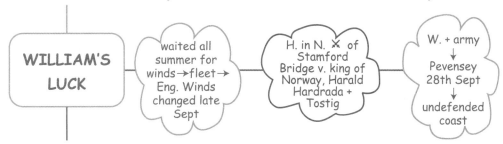

- **Third paragraph**: Look at the key words in the third paragraph. Can you think of a word or phrase that sums up the main idea in this paragraph? I suggest HAROLD'S ARMY. Draw a line down from your WILLIAM'S LUCK box to connect it with your third box. Now add your notes out to the side in the same way as before.

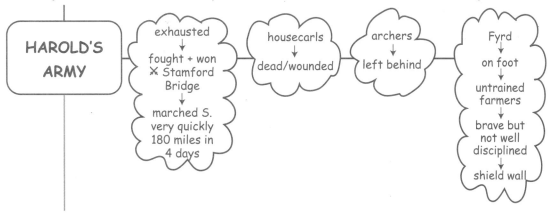

- **Fourth paragraph**: How about doing this one on your own? Here is my finished flow chart.

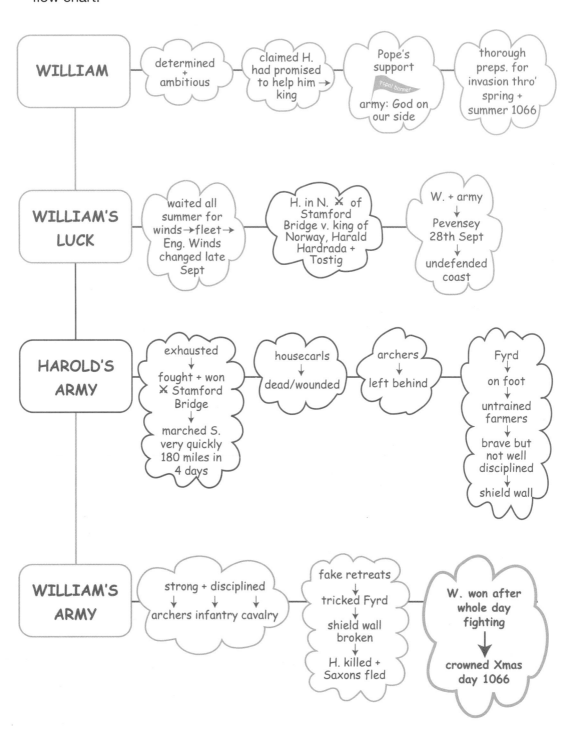

● Tips for making the most of flow charts
- Use colour to help group your notes. What about one colour for facts about William and another for facts about Harold? Fine liners or gel pens are good for this.
- You could use other shapes to draw round your notes: such as ovals or stars. Be creative.
- Revise from your flow charts in the same way that you would from your MIND MAPS® learning charts. Look at the tips on page 48.

I promise

Flow charts are good for any battle or rebellion where you describe the main events in the order in which they happened – for example the battles in the Hundred Years' War or the Peasants' Revolt.

Which topic will you use for your first box and bubble flow chart? .......................

.................................................................................................................

# 4.3 Index cards

This is a method that uses a question and answer approach with numbered points, key words, colour and pictures. Right-brain thinkers will enjoy using colour and pictures and left-brain thinkers will enjoy writing brief notes in numbered lists. We will make the most of all these things.

## Equipment you will need
- White or coloured index cards. 128 x 76 mm cards or 152 x 102 mm are best.
- Index box to store your cards in.
- Card dividers: each subject needs its own section. You can make your own.
- Good quality pens, fibre tips, fine liners or gel pens.

## Exercise 4.3: Creating a set of index cards
We will use a science topic – life processes. It does not matter if you have not studied this topic at school yet because you only need the information in the passage on page 55 for this first set of index cards.

**Step 1: Brain warm-up**
What do I already know about life processes?

Either jot down single words in a list or in a ring round the central bubble.

Life processes (as a list):

1. ...............................................
2. ...............................................
3. ...............................................
4. ...............................................
5. ...............................................

Or as a bubble chart:

Life processes

**Step 2: Key words**

What else do I want to know about life processes?

Read the passage below and find out more. Underline or highlight the key words. I suggest three colours: one for the main process, one for the detail to do with animals and a third for the detail to do with plants.

---

## Life processes

All living things have seven life processes in common. They can all do these things on their own. The seven processes are moving, respiring, sensing, growing, reproducing, excreting and nutrition.

Movement in animals means moving from place to place to find food. In plants it means moving towards a stimulus. A stimulus is a change that happens around an organism which makes it react in some way.

Respiration is a chemical process in which oxygen and food are changed into energy. All organisms need energy to grow and move. The waste products are water and carbon dioxide.

Living things use their senses to detect any changes in the environment. Sensitivity protects organisms from danger. Animals have several senses. Humans have five. These are sight, hearing, taste, smell and touch. Plants react to light, touch, temperature and gravity.

Growing is when living things become bigger. Animals grow until they are adults. Even when animals are fully grown they are continually replacing cells in their bodies as old ones die. Plants continue to grow until they die.

Reproduction is when living things produce offspring to keep the species going. Plants such as dandelions produce seeds in order to survive. Animals such as mammals have different numbers of young.

Excretion is when a living thing passes poisonous or unwanted material out of its body. Humans give out water and carbon dioxide when breathing, water in sweat and urine, and solid waste. Plants give out water and oxygen.

Nutrition is when living things take in food. Animals take in food to grow and to give them energy. Plants take in minerals and water. They use these together with carbon dioxide and sunlight to make their own food. This is called photosynthesis.

## Step 3: Into action

- Let's do this set of index cards together.

- **First card**: Write '1' in the top left hand corner of your first card. Number your cards one at a time. You will not know how many you are going to need until you have finished a topic.

- **Title**: What is this passage about? I suggest – LIFE PROCESSES. Write your title at the top of your first card in capital letters.

- **First paragraph**: Look at the key words in the first paragraph. How many points are made about life processes?

- **Front of first card**: Turn these points into questions or sub-headings and number them. I have turned all seven into a name: MRS GREN. This is a memory trick. You will find out more about these in section 4.5.

- **Back of first card**: Write your answers, numbering each point to match the numbers on the front. Use key words, abbreviations, pictures, colour and humour to make your answers memorable. Experiment and find out what works best for you.

- **Second card**: Write '2' in the top left-hand corner of your second card. Look at the key words in the second paragraph. Can you think of one word that sums up the main idea in this paragraph? I suggest MOVEMENT. Write this heading at the top of the card.

- **Front of second card**: How many points are made about moving? Turn these into questions or sub-headings. Number them. See how I have done mine.

- **Back of second card**: Write or draw your answers, numbering each point to match the numbers on the front.

- **Third card**: Write '3' in the top left-hand corner of your third card. Look at the key words in the third paragraph. Can you think of one word that sums up the main idea in this paragraph. I suggest RESPIRATION. Write this heading at the top of the card.

- **Front of third card**: How many points are made about respiration? Turn these into questions or sub-headings. Number them. See how I have done mine.

- **Back of third card**: Write or draw your answers, numbering each point to match the numbers on the front.

1.
### LIFE PROCESSES

MRS GREN?

1
2
3
4
5
6
7

WHAT?

Front

1  Moving
2  Respiring
3  Sensing
4  Growing
5  Reproducing
6  Excreting
7  Nutrition

All living things do all 7 on their own.

Back

2.
### MOVEMENT

WHAT?

1  Animals
2  Plants
3  Stimulus?

Front

1  Animals move place 2 place
2  Plants move 2 stimulus
3  Stimulus = change round an organism ➤ it reacts

Back

3.
### RESPIRATION

1  What?
2  Why?
3  Waste products (a)
              (b)

Front

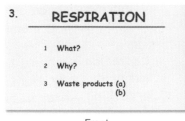

1. Chemical process: oxygen + food ➤ energy
2. All organisms need energy to groW + move
3. Water + $CO_2$

Back

- **Fourth card**: Write '4' in the top left-hand corner of your fourth card. Look at the key words in the fourth paragraph. Can you think of one word that sums up the main idea in this paragraph? I suggest SENSING. Write this heading at the top of the card.

- **Front of fourth card**: How many points are made about sensing? Turn these into questions or sub-headings. Number them. See how I have done mine.

- **Back of fourth card**: Write or draw your answers, numbering each point to match the numbers on the front.

How about doing the last four cards on your own? Remember to turn your information into questions on the front of your card and into answers on the back. Here are my final cards:

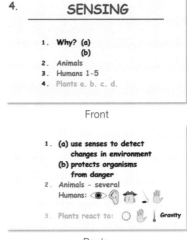

Front

Back

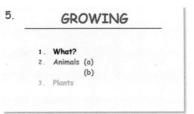

Front

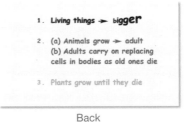

Back

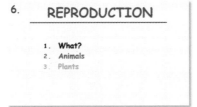

Front

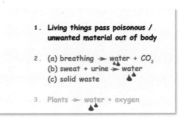

Back

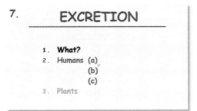

Front

Back

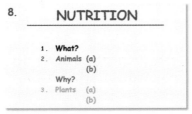

Front

Back

**Tips for making the most of index cards**

- The question/answer use of index cards is great for testing yourself. Set your cards out in a line in front of you, in order, question side upwards. See if you can give a full answer to each question. Turn the card over to check whether you have remembered all the points.

**If yes:**
Leave the card answer side upwards.

**If no:**
Turn it back over so you are looking at the questions again. Once you have been through all your cards, just test yourself again on the ones you did not know.

- **Visual learners:** Use different colours for different points. Enjoy using symbols and pictures.
- **Auditory learners:** Test yourself by giving full answers out loud or get a friend to test you.
- **Kinaesthetic learners:** Use the cards as actively as possible. Shuffle them, reorder them and see if you can still come up with the right answers.
- Choose which colour cards you want for each school subject. If you use white cards, colour code them with a dot in the top right-hand corner of each card so you know which subject it is part of.
- This method really helps you work on the facts you still need to learn without wasting time on the easy stuff that you already know.

---

**I promise**

Good science topics to try out on your own are food chains and food webs (life and living processes), the three states of matter (materials and their properties) or the eight types of energy (physical processes).

**1.** Which topic will you use for your first set of index cards? ...............................

**2.** What colour code do you promise to use? Fill in your colour code here for the subjects you want to revise using index cards.

| | | | |
|---|---|---|---|
| English | | Religious Studies | |
| Maths | | Latin | |
| Science | | Greek | |
| Life and living processes (biology) | | French | |

| Materials and their properties (chemistry) | | Spanish | |
| --- | --- | --- | --- |
| Physical processes (physics) | | German | |
| History | | Geography | |

## Take a break

You have made some more very important promises. Spend several weeks practising these three revision techniques before you move on.

## Which of the three revision techniques suits you best?

Give yourself a grade and carry on reading when you are happy with your score.

• I use MIND MAPS® learning charts:

   A all the time ☐   B most of the time ☐   C some of the time ☐   D never ☐

• I use box and bubble flow charts:

   A all the time ☐   B most of the time ☐   C some of the time ☐   D never ☐

• I use question/answer index cards:

   A all the time ☐   B most of the time ☐   C some of the time ☐   D never ☐

# 4.4 Numbered pegs

This revision technique is great when you need to know a list of facts in a particular order. You will learn to link the numbers one to ten with a set of rhyming words. Next you will link each number and rhyming word with a little story. These are the pegs you will hang your facts on. The most important thing you need for this technique is your imagination, so have fun!

## Equipment you will need
• A4 paper or a notepad to jot your ideas down on.
• A pencil.

## Exercise 4.4: Using numbered pegs
We are going to use a religious studies topic – the Ten Commandments. You do not need a passage for this but you will need someone in your back-up team to help you. First, your helper should teach you the numbered pegs. When you know these really well, he/she should read the stories on page 62 to you.

**Step 1: Learn the pegs**
Have a look at the numbered rhyming pegs below. Ask your helper to call out the number and the object while you concentrate on picturing and remembering them. Either keep your eyes closed or look up while you make as vivid a picture as you possibly can in your head.

**Numbered rhyming pegs**

| 1 = bun | | 6 = sticks | |
|---|---|---|---|
| 2 = shoe | | 7 = heaven | |
| 3 = tree | | 8 = gate | |
| 4 = door | | 9 = vine | |
| 5 = hive | | 10 = hen | |

Test yourself. You need to know the rhyming word that goes with each number really well.

**Step 2: Brain warm-up**
How many of the Ten Commandments do you know already?
Write them down here. If you know them in order, this is even better.

1. ...................................................................................................................

2. ...................................................................................................................

3. ...................................................................................................................

4. ...................................................................................................................

5. ...................................................................................................................

6. ...................................................................................................................

7. ...................................................................................................................

8. ...................................................................................................................

9. ...................................................................................................................

10. .................................................................................................................

**Step 3: Learn with the pegs**
Let's learn the Ten Commandments with the pegs. Ask your helper to read out the peg stories set out on the next page for the first five Commandments. Make a vivid picture in your head of the images. Your helper should test you on these. You do not need to tell him or her the stories. They are the pegs you hang the facts on. Just say the actual commandments. Once you have learnt the first five, then learn the last five. Your helper should test you again.

## Peg stories for the Ten Commandments

| | | | |
|---|---|---|---|
| **1.** | Bun | • Worship no god but me | Imagine you have just baked a most delicious **bun**, filled with fruit, jam and dripping with icing. You wish to give this bun to God, just the one true God, Yahweh. |
| **2.** | Shoe | • Do not make for yourself images to worship | You see a giant **shoe** filled with statues of all kinds of gods made of stone and wood. You sling them in the bin because you know you must not make statues of Yahweh or other gods. |
| **3.** | Tree | • Do not use the name of God for evil purposes | You are sitting on a branch of a **tree**. A ring of children is dancing round the tree shouting out rude names at you. You are very sad. Do not make fun of people's names, especially God's. |
| **4.** | Door | • Keep the Sabbath day as a holy day | You see a beautiful wooden **door** with carvings on it. There is a sign on the door with all the days of the week on it. The seventh day, the Sabbath, is printed in golden letters to remind Jews this is their day of rest. |
| **5.** | Hive | • Respect your father and mother | There is a large queen and king bee standing outside the **hive**. All the little bees are standing politely in a line in front of them. |
| **6.** | Sticks | • Do not commit murder | Some children are using **sticks** to kill butterflies in the garden. Their mother comes out, breaks up the sticks to stop them from killing and shouts at them very crossly. |
| **7.** | Heaven | • Do not commit adultery | A bride and groom are coming out of church. They look up to **heaven**. The sun is shining, they are very happy having just promised to be true to each other for the rest of their lives. |
| **8.** | Gate | • Do not steal | You see a robber stealing out of a house with a sack of stolen goods over his shoulder. As he gets to the **gate** he is taken by surprise as a large policeman comes up to arrest him. |

| 9. | Vine | • Do not accuse anyone falsely | You have a wonderful **vine** growing in your greenhouse. You see a little boy coming out of the greenhouse. He says he has not taken any grapes and that it was his brother that took them but you know he is lying because his T-shirt is covered in grape juice. |
| 10. | Hen | • Do not covet another person's property | You keep **hens** but you are very fed up because they do not lay many eggs. Your next door neighbour also has hens. His lay large brown eggs which he is very proud of. You feel cross and envious because you wish you had his hens. |

**Tips for making the most of rhyming pegs**

This is a great opportunity to put a reviewing routine into practice.

1. Learn the Commandments using the peg stories.

2. Take a five minute break. What are the good things to do in a short break? If you have forgotten, then check them out on page 20.

3. Review what you have learnt by writing the ten comandments below. Enjoy finding out how much better you know the Ten Commandments now.

1. ........................................................................................................

2. ........................................................................................................

3. ........................................................................................................

4. ........................................................................................................

5. ........................................................................................................

6. ........................................................................................................

7. ........................................................................................................

8. ........................................................................................................

9. ........................................................................................................

10. ........................................................................................................

**Step 4: Review routine for tough facts**
If your knowledge is still a bit shaky then review again a day later, a week later and a month later. These facts will then be in long-term memory and you will find them really easy to remember in tests and exams.

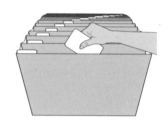

**Step 5: Other topics**
The good news is that you can use the pegs again for other topics. Wait until you know these facts really well and just make up a new set of stories for the next set of facts you need to learn.

You do not need to use ten pegs every time – just use the number you need.

I promise

How about using the pegs to learn the functions of a settlement for geography? You will only need the first six for this topic.

Which set of facts do you promise to learn using the pegs? ...............................

....................................................................................................................

# 4.5 Memory tricks

You will now find out even more about how to trick your brain into remembering by making unusual connections between facts and letters, words, pictures, rhymes and stories. Your brain loves these kinds of links. The best memory tricks are the ones you invent yourself, especially if they make you laugh. Once you understand how they work, start making up your own.

## Word and picture links

You can use all kinds of connections between the facts you want to learn and other words with a similar sound, an amusing meaning and much, much more. It is easier to demonstrate word and picture links rather than to explain them! They are fun to learn.

### Word and picture links for geography: Countries and capitals

Use blank playing cards. Write the country on one side and the capital on the other side of the card. Use a colour code. Have one colour for capitals in Europe, another colour for capitals in Africa and so on.

Here are some examples taken from the capitals of Europe:

The Netherlands

- Amsterdam, capital of The Netherlands. Underneath the words The Netherlands, draw a hamster next to a dam.

- Helsinki, capital of Finland.

Finland

Underneath the word Finland, draw a ship sinking in the red flames of hell.

The picture is the trigger to help you remember the name of the capital.

Have fun making up your own word and picture links. Just use this method for the capitals you have difficulty remembering – what I call tough facts.

### Word and picture links for languages

Use your blank playing cards for languages as well. What about using a colour code? You could write feminine vocabulary in pink, masculine in blue, neuter in brown (Latin and German).

Here is a word and picture link for 'bellum', Latin for war.

Bellum

Front

War

Back

### Word links for Latin
Make your memory tricks as amusing and personal as possible. A student called Nick came up with this memory trick for the order of cases in Latin.

| | |
|---|---|
| Nominative | Nick |
| Vocative | Vomits |
| Accusative | All over |
| Genitive | George's |
| Dative | Dinner |
| Ablative | Again |

## Letter links
See if the first letter of each word you want to learn makes another word or useful pattern. This is helpful when you need to learn a list in a particular order.

### Letter links for life processes
Here is the memory trick I used for life processes. The first letter for each process makes the name MRS GREN.

| | | | | |
|---|---|---|---|---|
| **M** | Moving | **G** | Growing |
| **R** | Respiring | **R** | Reproducing |
| **S** | Sensing | **E** | Excreting |
| | | **N** | Nutrition |

### Letter links for history
The first three Acts passed by Henry VIII to establish himself as Head of the Church give the letter links of ASS.

| | |
|---|---|
| **A** | Act of Appeals in 1533 |
| **S** | Act of Supremacy in 1534 |
| **S** | Act of Succession in 1534 |

Your brain loves stories so make one up that connects the facts together in a particular order. Ask someone in your back-up team to tell you this story for the Plagues of Egypt. Close your eyes or look up as you picture the story like a film in your head.

## Story for the Plagues of Egypt

Once upon a time God punished the Egyptians with ten terrible plagues. It all started when the river **Nile** turned to **blood**. Imagine how frightened the little **frogs** were as they hopped out of the river onto the bank. To their horror they met millions of **lice** crawling around all over the sand. Above them black clouds of **flies** were buzzing angrily in the air.

Things were to get even worse. **Animals** started dying of a **dreadful disease**. **People** were covered with huge **boils**. These really hurt when massive **hailstones** started falling from the sky. The storm brought out swarm after swarm of **locusts**. They filled the air and made everywhere **dark** for **three days**. Worst of all, the **first born son** in every family **died**.

## I promise

The best memory tricks are the ones that you make up yourself.

Which topic will you make up your own memory trick for? ....................................

## Take a break
You have made some more very important promises. Spend several weeks developing your memory tricks before you move on.

How are you getting on with memory tricks?
• Give yourself a grade and carry on reading when you are happy with your score.

• I use numbered pegs:

A all the time ☐   B most of the time ☐   C some of the time ☐   D never ☐

• I use memory tricks:

A all the time ☐   B most of the time ☐   C some of the time ☐   D never ☐

## Summary: Amazing revision techniques

Smart learners like lots of variety in their learning
They choose the revision techniques that suit them best.

• MIND MAPS® learning charts: You use colour, pictures and key words.
• Box and bubble flow charts: You write notes in boxes and bubbles linked together by lines and arrows.
• Index cards: You use numbered questions on one side of your cards with answers on the other.
• Numbered rhyming pegs: You link facts to stories connected to a number and an object.
• Memory tricks: You make unusual connections between facts and letters, words, stories or pictures.

# Advice about exams

An exam gives you the chance to show off your knowledge. Fantastic knowledge of all those facts you have been learning is very important, but you still need a few more skills to help you achieve those great grades.

In this chapter we will look at five skills you need in the actual exams.

## 5.1 Know what to expect

By the time your exams are approaching you should know the format of all the exams you will take in every subject you are studying. Are you an exam expert already? Find out by doing the next exercise.

### Exercise 5.1: Know what to expect
Choose a subject you will take an exam in: ...............................................................

How quickly can you answer the following questions?

**1.** How long does the exam last?...................................................................................

**2.** How many questions do I have to answer?................................................................

**3.** Do I get a choice?.....................................................................................................

**4.** What is the range of marks given to questions?.......................................................

Any hesitations? Yes? Then who is the member of your back-up team you should arrange a meeting with? Your teacher, of course. You should be able to answer the questions above quickly and easily for every subject.

Tips for smart learners
- Practice will help. Your teachers will give you lots of practice papers to do.
- Make sure you learn how to answer the questions in the last exercise for each subject.

# 5.2 Understand the instructions

Examiners use a special kind of language. It is much more formal than the language you use in everyday conversations. I call this 'top hat' language. You will be using what I call 'baseball cap' language in your day-to-day speech. You need to understand what this formal language means. You must also know the meanings of the instruction words that examiners use. Start by learning the meanings on the basic list. Put the tough words on to blank playing cards, the word on one side and the meaning on the other. Test yourself, then get someone in your back-up team to test you.

Discuss the main benefits of using this book

Is this book any good?

## Instruction words explained

### Basic list
You are very likely to meet these words in many exam papers:

| Compare | Show the similarities. |
|---|---|
| Contrast | Show the differences. |
| Describe | Give a full picture of your topic in words. |
| Discuss | Describe the important points for and against your topic. These could be advantages and disadvantages. Come to a conclusion of your own based on your assessment of the evidence you give for both sides of the argument. |
| Explain | Give reasons for, make clear. Give evidence to prove the points you make. |
| Explain the significance of | Explain why the topic is important, what effect it has or had. Give evidence to prove the points you make. |
| List | Give the reasons or points one by one. |
| Reasons, as in the instruction 'Give reasons to support your answer' | You must give evidence to prove the points you make. |
| Summarise | Give a brief account of the main points. |

**Extension list**
You may meet these words in some more advanced and Scholarship exam papers:

| | |
|---|---|
| Account for | Give reasons for the points you are making. |
| Analyse | Explore the main ideas of the topic. Show why they are important and how they are connected. |
| Assess | Consider the topic carefully and give a judgement on it. |
| Assessment, as in the instruction 'Is this a fair assessment of the topic?' | A statement has been made about the topic followed by this question. You have to decide whether the judgement/opinion given in the statement is a reasonable one. You must think carefully about the statement, decide where you stand and give evidence to show why you agree or disagree with the point of view given. |
| Comment on | Discuss the topic, explain it and give an opinion on it. |
| Criticise | Analyse and then make a judgement or give an opinion. You should show both the good and bad points of your topic. |
| Define | Give the meaning or definition of the topic. You should give examples to make the meaning clear. |
| Differentiate | Explore and explain the differences. |
| Distinguish | Explore and explain the differences. |
| Evaluate | Give an opinion about the importance or success of the topic you are writing about. |
| Interpret | Explain the meaning. You may need to refer to data as evidence or give examples and opinions. |
| Justify | Give good reasons for offering an opinion or reaching a conclusion. |
| Outline | Give the important facts and leave out the small details. |
| Relate | Show the links between things. |
| State | Give the main points. |
| Trace | Describe how something has developed in the order in which the events happened. Describe the causes and effects. |

# 5.3 Smart reading

You should now know the meanings of the main instruction words examiners use. The next step is to make sure you understand how they are being used in the actual exam questions. You will face many kinds of questions but here are four of the main categories you should learn to recognise:

Facts          Opinions          Reasons          Differences and Similarities

- **Fact** based questions: All that revision you have done will pay off now because you can show off your knowledge of the facts the examiner is asking for.
- **Opinion** based questions: You need to have your own views about the topic and be able to prove your opinion by giving evidence. You should choose the facts that support your opinion.
- **Reason** based questions: The examiner wants you to show that you know why something happened, or why it was a success or a failure, or why it was important. You should choose the facts that support your reasons.
- **Differences** and **Similarities** based questions: The examiner wants you to explain how aspects of your topic are either different or the same. These are the 'compare and contrast' questions and need very careful planning.

Remember the memory trick FORD/S

## Exercise 5.2: Smart reading
Read the following questions based on a history topic. Underline or highlight the important words in the questions. You could use the key word code. Here is a reminder of how it works.

| | |
|---|---|
| **Instruction/important** words | <u>Explain</u> |
| **Numbers** | one |
| **Names** · | <u>Hastings</u> |

Choose which category the questions belong in.  Write F for fact, O for opinion, R for reason or D/S for differences and similarities.

**A typical exam or Common Entrance question:**
1. From this period choose one battle in which the King or Queen of England was challenged for his or her throne, such as Hastings, Lincoln, Towton, Bosworth or another you have studied.

    (a) Describe the main events of the battle ..........

    (b) Explain the reasons why the challenger fought against the ruler ..........

**A Scholarship or more advanced exam question:**

**2.** How much did William I really control and change England?..........
Question based on the passage on page 50.

**3.** Describe the main differences between William's army and Harold's army at the
Battle of Hastings ..........

Answers: 1.(a) = F, 1.(b) = R, 2. = O, 3. = D/S

# 5.4 Writing good answers

You now understand what the examiner is asking you to do in the questions. The next
step is to get your answers down on paper in a way the examiner will enjoy reading.
Short answers should be straightforward, if your revision has been going well. It is the
long answers and the full essays that need more preparation.

## Watch out!

Let's start by looking at a bad answer to Q3 from the previous exercise. This question
is worth 8 marks. Always check how many marks a question is worth and follow this
important rule:

The higher the number of marks, the more detail you must give.

**Q3:** Describe the main differences between William's army and Harold's army at the
Battle of Hastings. [8 marks]

**Answer:**
Willam's army beat harald's in a tough battle in 1066. Loads of men got killed on
both sides willam won in the end. Harald's army was rubbish.
Examiner's mark: 0!

### Reasons why this is a bad answer
This is a pretty extreme example of a bad answer but there are some
mistakes in it you really do need to watch out for:
• I have not answered the question because I have not compared the two
armies. I have made one vague comment about Harold's but I have not gone on to
contrast his army with William's.
• I have spelled the names incorrectly. Harald was the king of Norway, so this is a very
bad spelling mistake.
• I have used casual or 'baseball cap' language.
• I have forgotten capital letters for names.

Let's look at a good answer to the same question and work out why it is better.

There were several important differences between William's army and Harold's at the Battle of Hastings. Firstly, William's army was fresh and keen for battle. They had been waiting all summer to set sail. On the other hand, Harold's was tired because they had just fought the Battle of Stamford Bridge and then marched all the way south in four days. Secondly, William's army was a better fighting force. It was made up of archers, infantry and cavalry. They were well disciplined. On the other hand, many of Harold's best fighters, the housecarls, were dead or wounded and he was forced to leave his archers behind. This left him with the Fyrd who were untrained farmers. Although they were brave, they were not very disciplined.
Examiner's mark: 8

**Reasons why this is a good answer**
- I have done what the examiner wanted me to do and actually answered his question!
- I have started with a lead-in sentence that uses words from the question and leads in (prepares for) the rest of my answer. This is worth doing at the beginning of all long answers.
- I have given a full explanation for my reasons with enough detail. I needed to do this to get good marks.
- I have used formal or 'top hat' language.
- I have used 'firstly,' 'secondly' and 'on the other hand' to guide the examiner through my answer. I call these signpost words because they show the examiner the direction I am going in, just like road signs.

Use signpost words to tell the examiner when you are about to start a new point. Here are a few more: Thirdly, Fourthly (and so on), Next, Finally, Lastly, Most importantly.

- I have spelled everything correctly and remembered capital letters for names.

It is vital that you spend a few minutes planning all long answers. How can you do this? Left-brain thinkers may like a simple, numbered list. Right-brain thinkers may like to draw a small MIND MAPS® learning chart. Find out which method works best for you and make sure you use some of the tips from above to help you write a good answer.

# 5.5 Final tips for examinations

● Before the exam

Are you at your best? You should:

- Make sure you have all your equipment ready the night before.
- Get a good night's sleep.
- Avoid last minute cramming as it is unlikely to help.
- Be determined: positive thinking is really important. Remember those goals you chose in Chapter 2.
- Be ready for two types of exam paper
  - Hard: don't panic. It's the same for everyone. Remember what happens to your brainpower if you get stressed!
  - Easy: be on your guard, avoid careless mistakes
- Do a relaxation exercise before going into the exam room so you are calm and ready to get all those facts from your thinking brain.

● During the exam

You should:

- Keep your watch on the desk so you can easily keep an eye on the time.
- Divide your time sensibly between all the questions – if a question is too tough for you, go on to the next one.
- Go back and have another go at those tough questions if you have time at the end.
- Check your answers if you have any more time at the end.
  Here are a few questions you could ask yourself at the end:
  - Do my answers make sense?
  - Have I spelled any long words or names that appear on the exam paper correctly?
  - Are any mathematical calculations I have carried out correct?

# 5.6 Make the most of feedback

How do you feel when you get the results of your tests or exams? Are you pleased, quite pleased or disappointed? Spend some time thinking about your test or exam results. Ask yourself the following questions:
• What did I do well?
• What do I need to improve next time?
• How will I achieve this?

Work out the answers so you know exactly how to keep on getting good grades or how to improve your grades.

## Exercise 5.3: Make the most of feedback ( www.galorepark.co.uk )
Use a feedback form to help you think through these important questions. Download as many copies as you need from the Galore Park website and use one for each subject.

Keep your feedback forms at the front of each subject file so you can check what action to take when you start preparing for the next tests or exams.

● Tips for making the most of feedback
• The better you know how and why you succeed, the more chance you have of boosting your grades next time.
• Listen to your teachers' advice. Make the most of their expertise.
• Discuss your feedback form with someone in your back-up team. They may have some useful suggestions to make about how you can boost your grades.

**Feedback Form**

Subject ....................................    Date of test/exam ..............................

How do you feel about your exam results?  Pleased, quite pleased or disappointed?
Put your marks in the column that matches how you feel about your result.  In the
next box put your reasons.  See notes 1 and 2.  In the next box put what action you
are going to take.

|  | 🙂 | 🙂 | 🙁 |
|---|---|---|---|
| Result: | | | |
| Reasons: | | | |
| Action to maintain/boost my grade next time: | | | |

**Note 1:** Possible reasons for being pleased: you love the subject; an easy paper; you
did a lot of revision; you read the questions really carefully and did what you were asked
to do.

**Note 2:** Possible reasons for being disappointed:  you ran out of time; you misread
some of the questions; you did both bits of an either/or question; you did not do enough
revision; it was a hard paper.

Now work out what kind of action to take for next time and take it!  You may feel that
all you need to do is carry on as you are doing already.

## I promise

How do you intend to become exam smart?

**1.** I shall ask my teachers the format of the exams.  Yes ☐ No ☐

**2.** I shall learn the meanings of key instruction words.  Yes ☐ No ☐

**3.** I shall <u>underline</u>/highlight key words in exam questions.  Yes ☐ No ☐

**4.** I shall use FORD/S to help me understand the questions.  Yes ☐ No ☐

**5.** I shall plan long answers and essays.  Yes ☐ No ☐

**6.** I shall use 'top hat' language in my answers.  Yes ☐ No ☐

**7.** I shall use feedback forms for the following subjects .........................................

.................................................................................................................

.................................................................................................................

How many of the seven promises above are you going to keep? .....................

## Take a break

You have made some more very important promises. You will need several weeks to become an exam expert.

## Are you exam smart?

How many of those seven important promises are you keeping?
I am keeping my promises:

A all the time ☐     B most of the time ☐     C some of the time ☐     D never ☐

Final feedback
Now check all your feedback scores.  Are you happy with them all?
**If no:**
Keep on working at those skills you still need to improve on.
**If yes:**

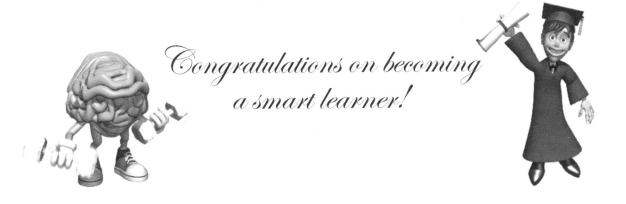

*Congratulations on becoming a smart learner!*

## Summary: Advice about exams

Smart learners are prepared for exams
- They know the format of the exam papers.
- They make sure they understand the questions.
- They plan long answers and full essays.
- They use 'top hat' language.
- They use time sensibly.
- They check their work at the end.
- They make the most of feedback from tests and exams.

# Recommended Reading

## The brain
*The Optimum Nutrition Bible by Patrick Holford* (2000) Judy Piatkus (Publishers) Ltd
*Music with the Brain in Mind* by Eric Jensen (2000) The Brain Store Inc
*Unicorns are Real – A Right-Brained Approach to Learning* by Barbara Meister Vitale (1994) Ann Arbor Publishing
*The Brain's Behind It* by Alistair Smith (2005) Crown House Publishing

## Memory
*Your Memory: A User's Guide* by Alan D Baddeley (2004) Carlton Books
*Use Your Head* by Tony Buzan (2006) BBC Worldwide Ltd
*Use Your Memory* by Tony Buzan (2006) BBC Active

## Motivation
*Tools for Engagement – Managing Emotional States for Learner Success* by Eric Jensen (2004) The Brain Store Inc
*The NLP Workbook* by Joseph O'Connor (2001) Thorsons

## Learning
*Accelerated Learning* by C Rose (1993) Accelerated Learning Systems Ltd
*Mind Maps for Kids – An Introduction* by Tony Buzan (2003) Thorsons
*The Learning Revolution* by Gordon Dryden and Jeannette Vos (2001) Network Education Press Inc.
*Righting the Educational Conveyor Belt* by Michael Grinder (1991) Metamorphous Press
*Strategies for Closing the Learning Gap* by Mike Hughes (2001) Network Educational Press Ltd
*Superteaching* Eric Jensen (1998) Brain Store Inc
*Mapping Inner Space* by Nancy Margulies (2004) Crown House Publishing
*The ALPS approach: accelerated learning in primary schools* by Alistair Smith and Nicola Call (2003) Network Educational Press Ltd

# Resources

From the Galore Park website www.galorepark.co.uk
Available as a download: Year planner (p31) , Weekly planner (p32), Topic checklist (p32), Subject checklist (p33) and Feedback form (p77).

## Workbooks
Writing skills, books A, 1, 2 and 3 by Diana Hanbury King (2nd edition) Educators Publishing Service Inc

## Equipment
Blank playing cards are available from:
Linney's Colour Print, Adamsway, Mansfield, Notts NG18 4FL tel. 01623 450 450
The Helen Arkell Centre, Frensham, Farnham, Surrey GU10 3BW tel. 01252 792400

## Computer programmes

The Mind Manager  www.mindjet.com/uk
Enables students to develop their ideas and present them in a MIND MAP® Learning Map format

## Inspiration

www.inspiration.com
Helps students brainstorm their ideas and group them in a range of visually appealing formats, in particular in a MIND MAP® learning chart.

## Time to Revise

www.calsc.co.uk or www.time2revise.co.uk
A computerised version of Jane Mitchell's concertina file reviewing method.

## Further website suggestions

www.alite.co.uk
Provides information about courses, publications and hands-on support to promote accelerated learning methods as defined by Alistair Smith.

www.arkellcentre.org.uk
Provides information about the range of services and professional training courses at the Helen Arkell Dyslexia Centre.

www.brainconnection.com
Provides information about how the brain works and how people learn.

www.innersense.info
Provides information about Inner Sense's range of Neuro-Linguistic Programming (NLP) courses.

# Notes

# Notes

# Notes

# Notes

# Notes